US MILITARY CAREERS

US NAVY

BY CARLA MOONEY

CONTENT CONSULTANTS
James C. Bradford
Professor Emeritus
Texas A&M University

Joseph T. Stanik
Lieutenant Commander (Retired)
US Navy

Essential Library

An Imprint of Abdo Publishing | abdobooks.com

ABDOBOOKS.COM

Published by Abdo Publishing, a division of ABDO, PO Box 398166, Minneapolis, Minnesota 55439.

Printed in the United States of America, North Mankato, Minnesota.
032020
092020

Cover Photo: Mass Communication Specialist 2nd Class Michael Eduardo Jorge/US Navy/ Defense Visual Information Distribution Service
Interior Photos: Mass Communication Specialist 3rd Class Scott Pittman/US Navy, 4–5; Mass Communication Specialist 3rd Class Connor Loessin/US Navy/Defense Visual Information Distribution Service, 7; Mass Communication Specialist 3rd Class Mar'Queon A. D. Tramble/US Navy/Defense Visual Information Distribution Service, 8; North Wind Picture Archives, 12–13, 15; Michael Dwyer/AP Images, 16; AP Images, 22; Mass Communication Specialist Seaman Apprentice Logan A. Southerland/US Navy/Defense Visual Information Distribution Service, 24–25; Mass Communication Specialist 2nd Class Manuel Tiscareno/US Navy/Defense Visual Information Distribution Service, 29; T. Whitney/Shutterstock Images, 31; Mass Communication Specialist 2nd Class Michael H. Lehman/US Navy/Defense Visual Information Distribution Service, 32, 65; Scott A. Thornbloom/US Navy, 36; Mass Communication Specialist 3rd Class John Grandin/US Navy, 38–39; Photographer's Mate 3rd Class Jay C. Pugh/US Navy/PJF Military Collection/Alamy, 43; Mass Communication Specialist 2nd Class Somers T. Steelman/ US Navy/Defense Visual Information Distribution Service, 46; Mass Communication Specialist 3rd Class Andrew Langholf/US Navy/Defense Visual Information Distribution Service, 50–51; Mass Communication Specialist 3rd Class Ashley E. Lowe/US Navy/Defense Visual Information Distribution Service, 55; US Navy/Defense Visual Information Distribution Service, 60–61, 68; Mass Communication Specialist 2nd Class Bobby J Siens/US Navy/Defense Visual Information Distribution Service, 70–71; Jacob Sippel, Naval Hospital Jacksonville/US Navy/Defense Visual Information Distribution Service, 75; Mass Communication Specialist 1st Class Scott Bigley/US Navy/Defense Visual Information Distribution Service, 80–81, 86; Chief Mass Communication Specialist Travis Simmons/US Navy/Defense Visual Information Distribution Service, 85; Mass Communication Specialist 1st Class Fred Gray IV/US Navy/Defense Visual Information Distribution Service, 90–91; Mass Communication Specialist 2nd Class Cameron Stoner/US Navy/Defense Visual Information Distribution Service, 94; Mass Communication Specialist 2nd Class Michael H. Lehman/US Navy, 98

Editor: Charly Haley
Series Designer: Nikki Nordby

LIBRARY OF CONGRESS CONTROL NUMBER: 2019954351

PUBLISHER'S CATALOGING-IN-PUBLICATION DATA

Names: Mooney, Carla, author.
Title: US Navy / by Carla Mooney
Description: Minneapolis, Minnesota : Abdo Publishing, 2021 | Series: US military careers | Includes online resources and index.
Identifiers: ISBN 9781532192302 (lib. bdg.) | ISBN 9781098210205 (ebook)
Subjects: LCSH: Navies--Juvenile literature. | Naval personnel--Juvenile literature. | Military power--Juvenile literature. | United States Navy--History--Juvenile literature. | Armed Forces--Juvenile literature.
Classification: DDC 355.12--dc23

CONTENTS

CHAPTER 1

RESCUE AT SEA

The rescue order came from a US Navy aircraft carrier. "There's an EA-6B Prowler in the water," the order said. The US Navy aircraft had crashed during routine exercises approximately 125 miles (200 km) off the coast of Southern California. Four people on board were stranded in the Pacific Ocean. In the rough waters, the downed flight crew members were in serious danger of drowning or dying from injuries

Navy rescue swimmers can be lowered into the water from helicopters or ships.

sustained in the crash. After a few minutes in the cold water, hypothermia would set in and could lead to death.

When the rescue call came in, a US Navy aviation rescue swimmer was ready. He was already in the air in a helicopter with three crew members, performing a training mission. The rescue swimmer had trained for hundreds of hours for a moment just like this one. Now it was time to put that training to use.

DIVING INTO DANGER

As the helicopter flew near the crash site, the navy rescue swimmer spotted the downed fliers. The helicopter hovered in the air, and its crew lowered the rescue swimmer in a hoist down to the choppy water. The wind whipped stinging sea spray into the swimmer's face while his eyes and nose were filled with the scent of jet fuel in the air and water.

Wearing a knee-length wet suit, the rescue swimmer swam through 10-foot (3 m) swells to the first two fliers, who were floating together. Weak and injured, the men were beginning to go into shock. The rescue swimmer grabbed the first man and swam with him back to the hoist. He hooked the man's rescue harness to the hoist, and the crew pulled the man into the helicopter. The rescue swimmer returned to bring the second man to the hoist, hooked him in, and watched as the crew pulled him safely into the helicopter.

The choppy waves and strong winds pushed the rescue swimmer at least 20 feet (6 m) away from the third flier. He pushed through the rough waters, adrenaline surging through his body. He reached the man and swam him back to the hoist. This time, the rescue swimmer rode with the injured flier as the hoist lifted them both into the helicopter. Yet his work was not done. There was still one more man in the water.

★ Navy helicopters can use large ships called aircraft carriers for takeoffs and landings.

The rescue swimmer descended once again into the cold water and swam to the last flier. Meanwhile, the helicopter flew away, carrying the injured men to the nearby navy aircraft carrier. On his own, the rescue swimmer loaded the unresponsive man into a small, one-person raft to wait for a

★ Rescue swimmers must work quickly, even in dangerous waters.

second rescue helicopter to arrive. While floating next to the raft, the rescue swimmer performed mouth-to-mouth resuscitation on the man. As he worked to save the man, a shark swam close by, attracted by the scent of blood in the water. The rescue swimmer did his best to ignore the dangerous animal as he waited for the second helicopter.

About 20 minutes later, the second helicopter arrived and lifted the last flier and the rescue swimmer to safety. The helicopter flew its passengers to the navy aircraft carrier, where the injured

ACTIVE DUTY VS. RESERVE

When joining the US Navy, recruits can choose to enter active duty, where they serve as full-time navy service members. Alternatively, they may choose to join the navy reserves and serve on a part-time basis. Navy reservists train one weekend per month and two full weeks per year while working in a civilian career. When needed, reservists may be called to active duty.

fliers received medical attention. After spending nearly an hour in the water, the rescue swimmer's body temperature had dropped sharply. He warmed himself with a long, hot shower and several cups of coffee.

Later, the rescue swimmer visited the men he had saved as they recovered in the hospital from broken bones and other injuries. In a US Navy tradition, the rescued men gave their names and unit patches to the swimmer who had saved them. The rescue swimmer proudly placed the patches on his gear bag. Although many people called him a hero, the rescue swimmer insisted that he was only doing his job.

MANY OPPORTUNITIES

The US Navy traces its origins to the formation of the Continental navy in 1775, when American colonists were fighting for independence from Great Britain. The navy defends the seas and protects the safety and interests of the United States, its citizens, and its allies. The US Navy trains, maintains, and

ENLISTED SAILORS

Most members of the US Navy start as enlisted sailors. Enlisted sailors must have earned a high school diploma or a GED. They are the general workforce of the navy, carrying out the navy's daily operations. They are often highly specialized and perform many hands-on tasks. There are hundreds of positions in dozens of job areas, from cryptology to nuclear operations, available for enlisted sailors. Joining the navy as an enlisted sailor is a binding commitment. Becoming an enlisted sailor generally requires a service commitment of four years. Some positions with longer training periods may require longer service commitments. Enlisted sailors cannot quit until they have fulfilled their commitment.

equips naval forces to fight and win wars, deter potential threats against the United States, and maintain freedom on the world's waters. In addition to defending the United States from sea-based threats, the navy also helps provide humanitarian aid when disasters strike around the world.

Many people are needed to keep the US Navy operating smoothly. As of 2019, the navy employed more than 330,000 active duty members and more than 100,000 reserve personnel.[1] Navy personnel operate, maintain, and repair ships and aircraft. They live and work on ships and submarines at sea, serve on naval aircraft on land and at sea, and serve at shore stations around the world. Each year, thousands of recruits join the navy and fill new positions and jobs left open by service members who have returned to civilian life.

The US Navy has more than 60 career fields from which to choose.[2] Service members can choose careers in communications or that are part of the flight operations team. They can work as navy nurses, nuclear operations technicians, or cryptologic technicians who decode intelligence information. With so many opportunities, a career in the navy can fit many backgrounds and interests.

COMMISSIONED OFFICERS

Some navy personnel are commissioned officers who have a four-year college degree and have completed officer training. Navy officers can either join as commissioned officers or be promoted to the officer ranks. Commissioned officers lead and manage enlisted personnel. There are many career fields available for officers, from health care to aviation to engineering. Generally, officers are required to have a bachelor's degree or higher, although highly trained technical specialists called warrant officers are not required to have a college degree. Becoming an officer generally requires a service commitment of three to five years, with some positions requiring longer service commitments.

CHAPTER 2

THE HISTORY OF THE US NAVY

The roots of the US Navy reach back as far as the American Revolutionary War (1775–1783). At the time, Great Britain's formidable Royal Navy ruled the sea, threatening colonial trade and coastal settlements. Some of the American colonies had established their own small navies to defend themselves, but

The first American naval forces were used during the Revolutionary War.

there was no national navy until the Continental Congress, which governed the colonies, formed the Continental navy in late 1775. The colonies' navies consisted of privateers, which were private ships hired by the colonial governments to prey on enemy ships. In September 1775, the colonists learned that two unarmed British ships carrying ammunition, weapons, and other supplies for British troops were sailing from Great Britain to Quebec. Without a national navy, General George Washington, who would later become the country's first president, chartered three private schooners to sail off the Massachusetts coast and intercept the enemy's supply ships.

In October 1775, General Washington urged the Continental Congress to form a national navy. In response, the Continental Congress voted to equip sailing vessels to prevent enemy ships from delivering supplies to British troops in America. Congress also established a committee that was responsible for purchasing, outfitting, manning, and operating the first ships of the Continental navy. On February 18, 1776, the first squadron of the Continental navy sailed to the Bahamas islands and returned with supplies captured from British forts. By 1777, the Continental navy had expanded to 31 ships.[1]

In 1779, Captain John Paul Jones led an American naval squadron on a cruise around the British Isles and defeated the British warship HMS *Serapis* off Great Britain's coast. At one point during the battle, the British captain asked Jones whether he was prepared to surrender. Jones responded with his iconic phrase, "I have not yet begun to fight."[2] After the Revolutionary War ended, Congress disbanded the Continental navy. The United States was once again without a navy.

ESTABLISHING THE US NAVY

Without a navy to protect them, American merchant ships were vulnerable to attack on the open seas. American merchants

★ Captain John Paul Jones was one of the most well-known American naval officers from the Revolutionary War.

sailing across the Mediterranean Sea to new trade markets were frequently attacked by North African pirates. When war broke out between Britain and France, privateers and warships of both of those nations began seizing American merchants for trading with the enemy. In order to protect the merchant ships, Congress

★ The USS *Constitution*, one of the US Navy's first commissioned warships, sails in 2017.

voted to reestablish a national navy in 1794 and authorized the construction of six ships. Three of these—the USS *United States*, the USS *Constellation*, and the USS *Constitution*—were launched in 1797.[3]

In 1798, President John Adams signed a congressional act that established the Department of the Navy. The new department would be responsible for all naval affairs. By the end of 1798, the US Navy included 14 completed vessels with many more being built.[4] Naval shipyards in Philadelphia, Pennsylvania; Boston, Massachusetts; New York City; and Washington, DC, emerged along the rivers and coastlines to produce naval ships and prepare them for service.

EARLY TESTS OF THE US NAVY

After the Revolutionary War, the British continued to attack American merchant ships. They also occupied American territory along the Great Lakes after the war and refused to leave. These aggressions led to the War of 1812 (1812–1814). Although the US fleet was much smaller than the British navy, several US Navy ships defeated British ships. The USS *Constitution* defeated the British vessel HMS *Guerriere* in August 1812 and HMS *Java* off the coast of Brazil in December. On the Great Lakes, the US Navy took control of Lake Erie. The US Navy also defeated the British on Lake Champlain, which blocked an invasion planned by the British army. This victory led to the war's eventual end with the signing of the Treaty of Ghent in December 1814.

EXPANDING THE FLEET

The US Navy's success in the War of 1812 led Congress to authorize the expansion of the naval fleet. Congress also gave the US Navy the responsibility of protecting overseas trade. Naval officials built hospitals near cities to support the growing navy. For example, in 1836, the Boston Naval Hospital opened as one of the first hospitals created specifically to treat naval personnel.

The American Civil War (1861–1865) began when Southern states seceded from the United States. The North set up a naval blockade along the coast to block ships from delivering supplies and communications to the South. The North also launched an emergency shipbuilding program. At the beginning of the war, the South controlled no naval ships. To build its naval force, the South acquired ships from Britain and captured Northern ships. The South also started its own shipbuilding program. By the time the Civil War ended, the US Navy had swelled to 671 ships,

US NAVAL ACADEMY

In 1845, Secretary of the Navy George Bancroft recognized the need for a school to formally train naval officers. He established the Naval School at Annapolis, Maryland. Its first class consisted of 50 midshipmen, which are the lowest-ranking officers, and seven professors. The midshipmen studied subjects such as mathematics, navigation, chemistry, English, philosophy, and French.

In 1850, the school became the US Naval Academy. Midshipmen studied at the academy for four years and trained on ships each summer. As the US Navy grew, so did the academy. In 1976, the academy began allowing women to enter as midshipmen.

Today, the academy is home to 4,000 midshipmen. The midshipmen take a core set of classes and can choose from 18 major fields of study, along with a variety of elective classes and research opportunities. Upon graduation, students earn a bachelor of science degree. With state-of-the-art academic and professional training, the academy prepares its midshipmen to become naval officers to lead the US Navy and its fleet.[5]

encompassing new ships from the North and South.[6] It had become the largest navy in the world.

After the Civil War, the United States halted shipbuilding until the 1880s, when it constructed four new vessels, the ABCD ships—USS *Atlanta*, USS *Boston*, USS *Chicago*, and USS *Dolphin*. In 1886, Congress authorized construction of the US Navy's first battleships, which are armored ships. One of these, the USS *Maine*, exploded in Havana Harbor in 1898, prompting the Spanish-American War (1898). After the war, the United States gained control over Puerto Rico, Guam, and the Philippines. To protect its growing power, the United States built new submarines, airplanes, battleships, and small ships called destroyers. When the United States entered World War I (1914–1918) in 1917, the country's expanded naval fleet was put into action.

AVIATION IN THE US NAVY

After World War I ended, the US Navy turned more of its attention to the air. Aviation was becoming increasingly important to naval operations. The navy built and developed aircraft carriers, which are large warships designed to serve as bases on which aircraft can take off and land. An aircraft carrier also includes radar technology and weapons to protect itself and surrounding ships from air attacks.

World War II (1939–1945) began in Europe when Germany invaded Poland. But when Japan, an ally of Germany, attacked the US Navy base at Pearl Harbor in Hawaii on December 7, 1941, the United States entered the war. The US Navy actively participated in combat in both the Pacific theater against Japan and the European theater against Germany and Italy. Throughout the war, the US Navy embarked on a massive construction program, building new planes, warships, aircraft carriers, merchant ships, and other vessels. It also expanded its number of officers and enlisted personnel from about 300,000 in 1941 to more than three million by the end of the war.[7]

Although many of the navy's battleships had been sunk in the Pearl Harbor attack, the navy's aircraft carriers remained mostly intact. The aircraft carriers became an important part of the navy's Pacific strategy. In the Pacific, the US Navy faced the Imperial Japanese Navy in several major battles. In the Battle of Midway in 1942, American aircraft carrier–based planes inflicted heavy damage on the Japanese fleet. The US Navy's victory in this battle served as a turning point in the war in the Pacific.

In Europe, one of the most important US Navy efforts of World War II occurred in June 1944. France, an ally of the United States, was being occupied by the German military. The US Navy provided amphibious ships, landing craft, and combat ships for the D-day landings on France's Normandy beaches.

PEARL HARBOR

On Sunday, December 7, 1941, Japan launched a surprise attack on the United States. Early in the morning, the first wave of planes took off from six Japanese carriers and headed for Pearl Harbor, a US naval base near Honolulu, Hawaii. The Japanese planes included torpedo bombers, dive-bombers, horizontal bombers, and fighters. Just before 8:00 a.m., the Japanese planes reached Pearl Harbor and unleashed a devastating attack. Less than two hours later, the attack was over. The US Navy had sustained heavy damage. Twenty-one ships of the US Pacific Fleet were damaged or sunk, including eight battleships. More than 300 aircraft were destroyed or damaged, most before they had a chance to take off. More than 2,000 Americans died in the attack and another 1,000 were wounded. The next day, President Franklin D. Roosevelt asked Congress to declare war on Japan.[8]

The successful D-day invasion was the first step in liberating France from Germany.

The navy's experiences in World War II proved that airpower, both land based and carrier based, was the future of the naval fleet. The navy built its force around fast-moving aircraft carriers, supported by smaller ships.

A NUCLEAR-POWERED NAVY

Recognizing the potential benefits of using nuclear energy for propulsion, naval engineer Hyman Rickover supervised the construction of the USS *Nautilus*, the first nuclear-powered submarine. It launched in January 1954, meaning its construction was completed at that time. It was commissioned eight months later, in September 1954, meaning the navy declared the vessel ready for active service. The *Nautilus* was

★ The US Navy's USS *Nautilus*, which was the world's first nuclear-powered submarine, traveled under the North Pole in 1958.

large, about 323 feet (98.5 m) long. It was also fast and could move at 22 knots (41 kmh) on the surface and 23 knots (43 kmh) underwater.[9] The submarine could cruise for 50,000 miles (80,000 km) without refueling.[10] The *Nautilus* and other early nuclear submarines were the fastest underwater ships in the world. With its speed, ability to stay underwater for long periods, and sonar to track enemy ships, the nuclear submarine was well equipped to maneuver, track, and destroy its targets.

After the development of the USS *Nautilus*, the US Navy launched research into nuclear power for surface vessels. The USS *Enterprise*, the navy's first nuclear-powered aircraft carrier, was launched in September 1960 and commissioned in November 1961.

SUPPORTING ARMED CONFLICT

In the years since World War II, the US Navy has supported the overall US military strategy in conflicts around the world. The navy's sailors fought during the Korean War (1950–1953) and the Vietnam War (1954–1975). Naval ships were used to blockade Cuba during the Cuban missile crisis in October 1962. In 1991, the US Navy helped liberate Kuwait from an invasion of Iraqi forces and launched strikes from navy aircraft carriers in the Persian Gulf War (1990–1991). In the early 2000s, the US Navy provided a base for air operations for US forces during invasions of Afghanistan and Iraq.

Today, the US Navy is one of the most technologically advanced armed forces in the world. Its sailors support US armed forces in conflicts and humanitarian missions around the globe.

ORIGIN OF ENSIGN

The US Navy's lowest-ranking officers are called *ensigns*. This name originated in medieval times. Medieval lords honored some squires by allowing them to carry a banner called an ensign into battle. Soon, the squires became known simply by the ensign name. In the US Army, the lowest-ranking officer was originally called an ensign because, like the medieval squire, he was training to lead men into battle. The US Navy also adopted this tradition and assigned the rank of ensign for its junior commissioned officers.

CHAPTER 3

THE US NAVY TODAY

Today, the US Navy is the largest navy in the world. It is one of the six branches of the US military, along with the US Army, US Air Force, US Marine Corps, US Coast Guard, and US Space Force. As of January 2020, the navy had approximately 338,000 active duty personnel, with an additional 103,700 reserve members as of December 2019.[1] The navy is the branch of the military responsible for providing the United States' naval

Almost all navy personnel spend part of their career serving on board a ship.

power, along with the coast guard. The navy has a significant portion of the US military's airpower, too. The US Navy is organized into two main branches: shore establishment and operating forces. Sometimes these branches overlap.

The shore establishment is the administrative branch of the US Navy. It provides support to the operating forces. This includes providing fuel, ammunition, and other supplies. The shore establishment also manages the repair and maintenance of ships, aircraft, machinery, and electronics. This branch also handles training and educating naval personnel, including through the US Naval Academy. The shore establishment operates the navy's communications centers and provides intelligence and meteorological support to the operating forces. It also manages US Navy medical and dental facilities and air bases.

NAVY SEABEES

US Navy construction battalions, also known as Seabees, are the construction force of the navy. Since their formation during World War II, the Seabees' motto has been We Build, We Fight. They build navy bases, roadways, airstrips, and any other infrastructure the navy needs. The Seabees have built projects during conflicts and wars in Korea, Vietnam, Afghanistan, Kuwait, and Iraq. Primarily land based, the Seabees are trained in several construction and engineering skills. They work as builders, engineering aides, steelworkers, electricians, plumbers, mechanics, masons, equipment operators, and in other construction jobs.

OPERATING FORCES

The operating forces branch of the US Navy carries out specific missions and exercises, such as providing security and escorting US vessels in various regions of the world. The operating forces are divided into nine commands. These are the Atlantic Fleet (also known as Fleet Forces Command), the Pacific Fleet, Naval Forces Europe, Naval Forces Central Command, Naval Forces Southern Command, US Fleet Cyber Command, the US Naval Special Warfare Command, the US Navy Reserve, and the Operational Test and Evaluation Force.

The Atlantic Fleet operates in the Atlantic Ocean, while the Pacific Fleet operates in the Pacific and Indian Oceans. Naval Forces Europe is responsible for operations in the Mediterranean and Black Seas. Naval Forces Central Command's primary area of responsibility is the Middle East, including the Persian Gulf, Red Sea, and parts of the Indian Ocean. Naval Forces Southern Command's area of responsibility includes South America, Central America, the Caribbean Sea, and the surrounding waters. US Fleet Cyber Command is responsible for the navy's information networks, cyber operations, and cyber security. The US Naval Special Warfare Command is in charge of the navy's special missions and operations, while the US Navy Reserve holds the navy's reserve force, which is called into active duty only when needed. The Operational Test and Evaluation Force provides independent and objective testing of the navy's equipment, systems, and tactics.

MILITARY SEALIFT COMMAND

Military Sealift Command (MSC) is a special part of the navy. This command conducts seaborne transportation of supplies for every branch of the US military. Military Sealift Command carries dry goods, fuel, and other critical supplies on massive cargo ships and tankers to sites around the world, wherever the US military needs them. The command also transports combat cargo and conducts special missions. Employees of the MSC are not active duty members of the military but rather civilian employees.

Within each operating forces command, numbered fleets operate in a specific geographic area. The number of active fleets can vary from year to year. As of 2019, the US Navy had seven active fleets around the world.[2] Each fleet has a group of ships, submarines, and aircraft assigned to it.

Every ship, submarine, and aircraft in the US Navy has specific functions and strengths. They rarely operate alone. Instead, a group of vessels and aircraft work together in task forces on specific missions. Some fleets have specially grouped ships, such as a carrier group or strike group, assigned to work together on missions. The largest and most powerful unit in the navy is a carrier strike group. This group includes an aircraft carrier, its associated aircraft, and a group of accompanying ships.

NAVY RANKS

Navy sailors generally fall into three main categories: enlisted sailors, warrant officers, and commissioned officers. Enlisted sailors are the main workforce of the navy. When a recruit joins the US Navy as an enlisted sailor, he or she starts at the rank of seaman recruit. After completing recruit training, the enlisted sailor advances to the rank of seaman. As enlisted sailors gain experience, they can earn promotions to higher ranks, which come with more pay. The highest enlisted rank is master chief

★ The navy holds ceremonies to promote sailors or officers to higher ranks.

petty officer of the navy, a senior noncommissioned officer. Along with a rank, each navy sailor has a rating, which is his or her specific job in the navy.

Experienced chief petty officers can be commissioned and promoted to become navy chief warrant officers. Navy chief warrant officers are technical specialists who have knowledge and skills beyond the highest enlisted rank. There are four chief warrant officer ranks.

Commissioned officers have earned at least a four-year degree from a college or university and have completed officer training. The most junior commissioned officer is an ensign. Experienced officers can earn promotions to higher ranks such as lieutenant or captain. There are ten officer ranks as well as the rank of fleet admiral, which is reserved for wartime only.

No matter which rating, or job, a service member has in the navy, the ranking structure is the same. A service member's pay depends on his or her rating and years of service. Promotion opportunities are based on performance. Enlisted sailors who earn a bachelor's degree can be promoted to commissioned officers.

NAVY SHIPS AND AIRCRAFT

The US Navy has a variety of ships under its command that operate from bases around the world. As of January 2020, the

US NAVY RANKS

ENLISTED SAILORS

Seaman Recruit
Seaman Apprentice
Seaman

NONCOMMISSIONED OFFICERS (ENLISTED)

Petty Officer Third Class
Petty Officer Second Class
Petty Officer First Class
Chief Petty Officer
Senior Chief Petty Officer
Master Chief Petty Officer
Fleet/Command Master Chief Petty Officer
Master Chief Petty Officer of the Navy

WARRANT OFFICERS

Warrant Officer 1
Chief Warrant Officer 2
Chief Warrant Officer 3
Chief Warrant Officer 4
Chief Warrant Officer 5

COMMISSIONED OFFICERS

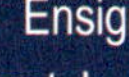

Ensign
Lieutenant Junior Grade
Lieutenant
Lieutenant Commander
Commander
Captain
Rear Admiral Lower Half
Rear Admiral Upper Half
Vice Admiral
Admiral
Fleet Admiral

★ Cruisers, such as the USS *Normandy*, are some of the smaller ships in the navy's fleet.

navy had 293 ships with 250 that were active in commission.[3] The most well-known navy vessels are aircraft carriers, submarines, and destroyers. However, there are several other types of smaller ships that are an essential part of the navy's force. Each type of ship has its own function and role in the navy's operations.

Aircraft carriers are the navy's largest ships. These ships are like floating cities and carry a crew of about 5,500, including about 2,000 navy airmen.[4] Aircraft carriers carry the navy's fighter aircraft. On the carrier's deck, a runway allows the aircraft to take off and land. Each carrier transports about 80 aircraft.[5]

Cruisers and destroyers are smaller, multipurpose ships usually deployed in a supporting role as part of a carrier group or an amphibious assault group. Armed with advanced guided missile systems, which can control the direction of a missile while it is in the air, cruisers can be used to defend against enemy aircraft. Similarly, destroyers defend against enemy submarines and ships. Equipped with several weapons, destroyers are also capable of defending against attacks by land or air.

Stealthy submarines operate underwater and can patrol for up to six months without surfacing.[6] They carry a number of weapons. The navy can use submarines to fire missiles at enemy targets. Submarines can also be used for surveillance.

Support ships provide navy forces with necessary supplies and provisions. They carry fuel, food, repair parts, mail, and other items. Some ships supply ammunition, while others

MILITARY ENTRANCE PROCESSING STATION

Each person who wants to join the US Navy must first go through the Military Entrance Processing Station (MEPS). MEPS ensures that all new members of the navy and other branches of the US military meet the mental, moral, and medical standards required by the US Department of Defense. There are 65 MEPS locations across the United States. At a MEPS location, applicants take a career aptitude test. They complete an extensive medical exam, including a weight check, hearing test, and vision test. They work with a service counselor to select a military job and participate in a pre-enlistment interview to highlight any potential legal issues that could prevent enlistment. Once it is determined that the applicant is qualified to enlist, he or she takes the oath of enlistment. The new recruit then prepares to report to basic training.

operate as rescue and salvage vessels, tankers, or tugboats. Used during wartime and natural disasters, hospital ships are like floating hospitals complete with emergency rooms, operating rooms, beds for patients, nurses, doctors, and dentists. The navy also uses a variety of smaller ships and boats for special purposes. Coastal patrol boats, oceanographic survey ships, surveillance ships, and special operations boats are just some of these vessels.

The navy's aircraft are used in combat and for transport. Navy aircraft must be able to operate from the deck of an aircraft carrier. Thus, they must be able to take off and land on a fairly short runway. Powerful catapults help them launch from carriers, and arresting wires are used to slow them down when landing.

Naval aircraft must be strong and sturdy to withstand these sharp, sudden forces.

LIFE IN THE NAVY

The primary focus of life in the US Navy is living and working on a ship. Sailors are typically assigned to a ship for a three-year period.[7] Sometimes, the ship is docked at its home port. Other times, it is deployed at sea. Navy ships are typically deployed for six to nine months and can travel all over the world.[8]

Navy sailors experience a variety of work environments. They study in academic classrooms and train on ships. They are assigned to duties on shore and at sea. On a ship, they perform specialized duties in their assigned area, such as on a flight deck. There is always a lot of work to be done on a navy ship, so sailors stay busy. Each day is broken into shifts. During each shift, a sailor may be performing job-related tasks, standing watch, or enjoying free time with shipmates. For those who enjoy adventure, a navy career can be very rewarding. US Navy personnel are stationed all over the world.

WELCOME TO BASIC

BOOT CAMP TO BATTLE STATIONS 21

All navy enlisted recruits attend recruit training, also known as basic training or boot camp. When recruits arrive, they are placed into divisions and assigned a commander. During the first week, recruits fill out forms, have medical and dental exams, receive vaccinations, and have their hair cut.

Once that processing week is complete, training begins. Over the next six weeks, recruits take classes on a variety of topics, from naval history to military customs. Recruits also have hands-on training in marksmanship, seamanship, water survival, and firefighting. Recruits have little free time during these intense training days. Throughout training, the recruit divisions compete with each other.

At the end of the seventh training week, recruits must pass a final evaluation called Battle Stations 21. This 12-hour event tests a recruit's physical fitness, knowledge of naval history, commitment to the team, and ability to apply skills learned in recruit training. Recruits who pass the evaluation receive a navy ball cap to replace the recruit ball cap they wore throughout training. This signals that a recruit has earned the right to be a sailor in the US Navy.

Recruit training ends with Pass-In-Review, a formal military ceremony that honors the recruit's hard work and dedication. Family and friends are invited to celebrate recruits' graduation from training. After completing training, each new sailor moves on to one of several jobs in the navy.

★ Navy recruits line up and are inspected by officers.

CHAPTER 4

AVIATION RESCUE SWIMMER

As a teenager, Jamison Ware worked as a lifeguard for Okaloosa County Beaches in Florida. Although he was a strong swimmer with lifesaving skills, Ware did not think his experiences on the beach would lead to a career he loves. "I got great pride from lifeguarding, but I never for one second

A helicopter lowers a US Navy aviation rescue swimmer into the misty sea.

thought I would ever have a career rescuing people from the water," Ware says.[1] When a friend encouraged him to explore a career in the US Navy as an aviation rescue swimmer, Ware was intrigued. "It just seemed like something I could be good at," he says.[2] After talking to a navy recruiter, Ware enlisted in the navy and passed the grueling training to become a naval aviation rescue swimmer. Throughout his career, Ware has performed countless search-and-rescue missions. Every day, he strives to live by the motto of the aviation rescue swimmers: So Others May Live. He does this by helping others in dangerous situations. "If you think about yourself first, you shouldn't be an air rescue swimmer. It's about total unselfishness . . . putting your life on the line so others can go home to their friends and families. There is nothing more gratifying than helping out someone in need," he says.[3]

ON THE JOB

US Navy aviation rescue swimmers (AIRRs) perform search-and-rescue missions from helicopters. Every day, AIRRs must be prepared to enter dangerous conditions to help others in need. AIRRs may be asked to jump or rappel out of a helicopter into the ocean to save the crew of a downed aircraft. They put

SURFACE RESCUE SWIMMER

Some rescue swimmers in the navy, called surface rescue swimmers, are based on a ship. Instead of jumping from a helicopter like AIRRs, surface rescue swimmers are lowered into the water by a cable from the ship or deployed in a small boat. For Damage Controlman Second Class Seth Witthaus, becoming a navy surface rescue swimmer seemed like a perfect fit. Witthaus grew up boating and swimming in Missouri's rivers and lakes. When he first enlisted, Witthaus was assigned to the USS *Oscar Austin*, a guided missile destroyer, and worked as a damage controlman, which is a type of emergency repair specialist. When there was an opening for a rescue swimmer on the ship, Witthaus applied. After being accepted, he spent weeks in intense training before returning to the *Oscar Austin* as one of the ship's two surface rescue swimmers. "I like helping people, so that was the ultimate goal," he says.[4] Witthaus has traveled around the world on navy missions.

their own lives in danger to save people on stranded or capsized vessels at sea or hikers and mountain climbers in danger on land. Sometimes, they partner with the coast guard or other military forces to rescue people during natural disasters such as hurricanes and tsunamis.

According to Naval Aircrewman Second Class Adam Trump, rescue swimming is much more difficult than jumping into the water and pulling someone out. Rescue swimmers must learn to time their dives so they are not overwhelmed by waves as high as 25 feet (7.6 m). Once in the water, the challenges continue. "With downed aircraft, you have to disentangle aviators, and a lot of things are covered in fuel, making for explosive hazards," Trump says. "If someone parachutes out, you have to separate them from their harness."[5] Trump, who is stationed at Naval Air Station Whidbey Island in Oak Harbor, Washington, has been called for both military and civilian rescue missions on water and land. In addition to jumping into rough seas, he has used hoists and rappelling gear to navigate mountains and trees that tower hundreds of feet into the air. "We've had sketchy situations where we're trying to load someone into our helicopter, but we can only set one wheel of the helicopter on the side of a cliff," says Trump.[6]

Life as an AIRR is unpredictable. AIRRs usually don't know when or where they will be called to work. "We've been sent to [evacuate] people from the San Juan Islands at 3 in the morning," Trump says. "Just recently, we went to Mount Baker." Another day, Trump's team pulled seven children and two adults out of Deception Pass, a strait that separates Whidbey Island from Fidalgo Island in Washington State. "On average, our unit winds up saving about three people a week," says Trump.[7]

AIRRs also provide humanitarian aid and operational support. They deliver supplies to other countries as part of humanitarian missions. They support Naval Special Warfare Operations and the Navy SEALs in a variety of covert combat missions. They also conduct surveillance in anti-submarine warfare operations, and they transport troops and cargo to and from ships with their helicopter teams.

ARMED SERVICE VOCATIONAL APTITUDE BATTERY

All military recruits take the Armed Service Vocational Aptitude Battery (ASVAB) when they enlist. The ASVAB is a multiple-choice test developed by the Department of Defense that measures a recruit's strengths, weaknesses, and potential for future success in the military. It consists of several subtests in subjects such as science, arithmetic reasoning, word knowledge, electronics, and mechanical comprehension. The goal of the test is twofold: to determine whether a recruit has the mental aptitude to enlist and succeed in a specific military branch and to help the military determine which careers the recruit is well-suited to pursue. The maximum ASVAB score is 99. The navy requires a minimum score of 35 for enlistment. Some navy careers require other specific ASVAB scores.

★ A US Navy aviation rescue swimmer pulls a person from a Louisiana rooftop into a helicopter in the aftermath of Hurricane Katrina in 2005.

WORK ENVIRONMENT

AIRRs can work anywhere in the world, helping anyone in need. They might be called to rescue the crew of a ship sinking in the Atlantic Ocean, sent to help survivors of a fierce hurricane in the Caribbean, or flown in to save an injured mountain climber stranded on a hard-to-reach cliff. They travel all over the world on humanitarian missions to provide support and supplies. Whatever the situation or location, AIRRs must be prepared to take action.

AIRRs can be assigned to duty on sea or shore. They are assigned to squadrons at naval air stations. Typically, AIRRs deploy into the field on aircraft carriers, other warships, and support ships. Petty Officer Second Class Melissa Dixon is

NAVY SPECIAL OPERATIONS

Navy AIRRs are part of the Naval Special Warfare (NSW)/Naval Special Operations (NSO) community that includes Navy SEALs, explosive ordnance disposal technicians, special warfare combat-craft crewmen, and navy divers. To qualify for any of these careers, recruits must have top academic scores as well as superior physical and mental stamina. When they enlist, recruits interested in NSW/NSO jobs meet with NSW/NSO coordinators. The recruits must also take the Computerized Special Operations Resilience Test (C-SORT), along with a physical screening test. The C-SORT assesses a recruit's personality and their ability to work in difficult environments and stressful conditions. The scores of the C-SORT and physical screening tests are combined to determine whether a recruit qualifies to enter an NSW/NSO career.

another aviation rescue swimmer stationed at Naval Air Station Whidbey Island. She performs search-and-rescue missions in the area's bays and oceans. She also performs missions in the nearby Olympic Mountains and the Cascade Mountains. "As a rescue swimmer, my core responsibility is to help anyone that's in distress," she says.[8]

QUALIFICATIONS AND EDUCATION

US Navy AIRRs are enlisted sailors. As such, they are required to have a high school diploma. Because the job of an AIRR is extremely physically demanding, those interested in this career must meet certain physical standards. To qualify for rescue swimmer training, which comes after recruit training, a person must have vision that is correctable to 20/20 in both eyes with normal depth perception and color perception. AIRR training program candidates must also be able to swim 500 yards (457 m) in 12 minutes, run 1.5 miles (2.4 km) in 12 minutes, do 42 push-ups in two minutes, perform 50 sit-ups in two minutes, perform four pull-ups, and pass a physical fitness screening test. Once candidates successfully complete these requirements, they can begin AIRR training.

For people considering an AIRR career, Dixon suggests getting into top physical condition. "A rescue swimmer [should]

Navy rescue swimmers train in many different environments, including in swimming pools. ★

be physically fit. We do a lot of things; we do tons of swimming. So, lots of endurance. Being able to carry people, being able to be out in the elements for longer than you usually would be. If someone needs help, and they can't help themselves, I'm there, and I can help them and get them home safe," she says.[9]

TRAINING AND ADVANCEMENT

Once they meet the basic physical requirements and are accepted into the AIRR training program, candidates must complete nearly two years of training in advanced swimming and lifesaving techniques. They also learn how to use equipment for helicopter missions, and they train on weapons systems.

MAKING AN IMPACT

When people are in danger, the navy's aviation rescue swimmers bravely put their own safety at risk to save others. They are some of the world's top emergency responders, jumping into action wherever and whenever they are needed. On March 25, 2019, a rescue team from Naval Air Station Whidbey Island in Washington State received an alert at 1:30 p.m. There was a stranded boater sitting on an overturned boat near Possession Point off South Whidbey Island. Within 15 minutes, the five-person rescue team took off in a helicopter. They arrived at the scene by 1:58 p.m.[10] An AIRR brought the man aboard the helicopter, which flew him to a local hospital for further evaluation. The rescue of the stranded boater is just one example of the many times navy AIRRs demonstrate their bravery and make an impact in the world.

The tough, realistic training is designed to prepare AIRRs to operate in any challenging environment they may encounter. As training progresses, the scenarios become more challenging and difficult, designed to test candidates both physically and mentally.

AIRR candidates begin specialized training at Aircrew Candidate School in Pensacola, Florida, where they learn water and land survival and flight safety skills over four weeks. Upon successful completion, they move on to five weeks of search-and-rescue swimming skills training at Rescue Swimmer School and 14 weeks of basic naval aviation skills at Class "A" Technical School. Then, AIRR candidates learn survival, evasion, resistance, and escape (SERE) techniques at SERE School. Finally, they spend an average of 28 weeks at a naval air station to train on aircraft systems.

Upon graduation from the program, AIRRs may be assigned to a helicopter command at sea or on shore in various places across the United States. Some AIRRs receive advanced training in emergency medical technician (EMT) skills. Some attend Advanced Rescue Swimmer School, where they train to handle swift water, high seas, and cave and cliff rescues.

TOP FIVE QUESTIONS

WHAT IS IT LIKE TO WORK AS AN AVIATION RESCUE SWIMMER?

AIRRs must be prepared to enter the most treacherous conditions to save those in need. They might jump or rappel out of a helicopter into the ocean. They may fly to a mountain cliff to rescue a stranded hiker. For an AIRR, every day brings a new and often dangerous challenge.

WHAT SHOULD THOSE WHO ARE INTERESTED IN THIS CAREER STUDY IN SCHOOL?

AIRR candidates should take as many physical education classes as possible in high school. They should also take English, mathematics, and basic science courses to prepare for the Armed Service Vocational Aptitude Battery (ASVAB) exam, which they will take upon enlistment.

WHAT SKILLS ARE BENEFICIAL FOR THOSE INTERESTED IN THIS CAREER?

AIRR candidates should be in top physical condition. They should have superior swimming skills. They should also be able to remain calm and work under pressure.

WHAT IS THE TYPICAL SALARY FOR AN AIRR?

In the navy, basic pay is based on a service member's rank and years of service. As of January 2019, the base salary for active duty enlisted service members ranged from $20,172 (ranked with less than two years of service) to $98,904 (ranked with more than 38 years of service).[11] In addition to basic pay, AIRRs are eligible for enlistment bonuses and special duty assignment pay.

AFTER SERVING IN THE NAVY, WHAT CIVILIAN CAREERS ARE AIRRS QUALIFIED FOR?

AIRRs are typically valued for their leadership skills, self-determination, and organization. After the navy, AIRRs can use these skills in a variety of careers, from high-level security consulting to emergency medicine.

CHAPTER 5

NUCLEAR OPERATIONS TECHNICIAN

The US Navy operates numerous nuclear-powered submarines and aircraft carriers. On board nuclear-powered vessels, a nuclear power plant provides energy for almost everything the vessel and its crew does. The nuclear power plant provides the energy needed to propel the

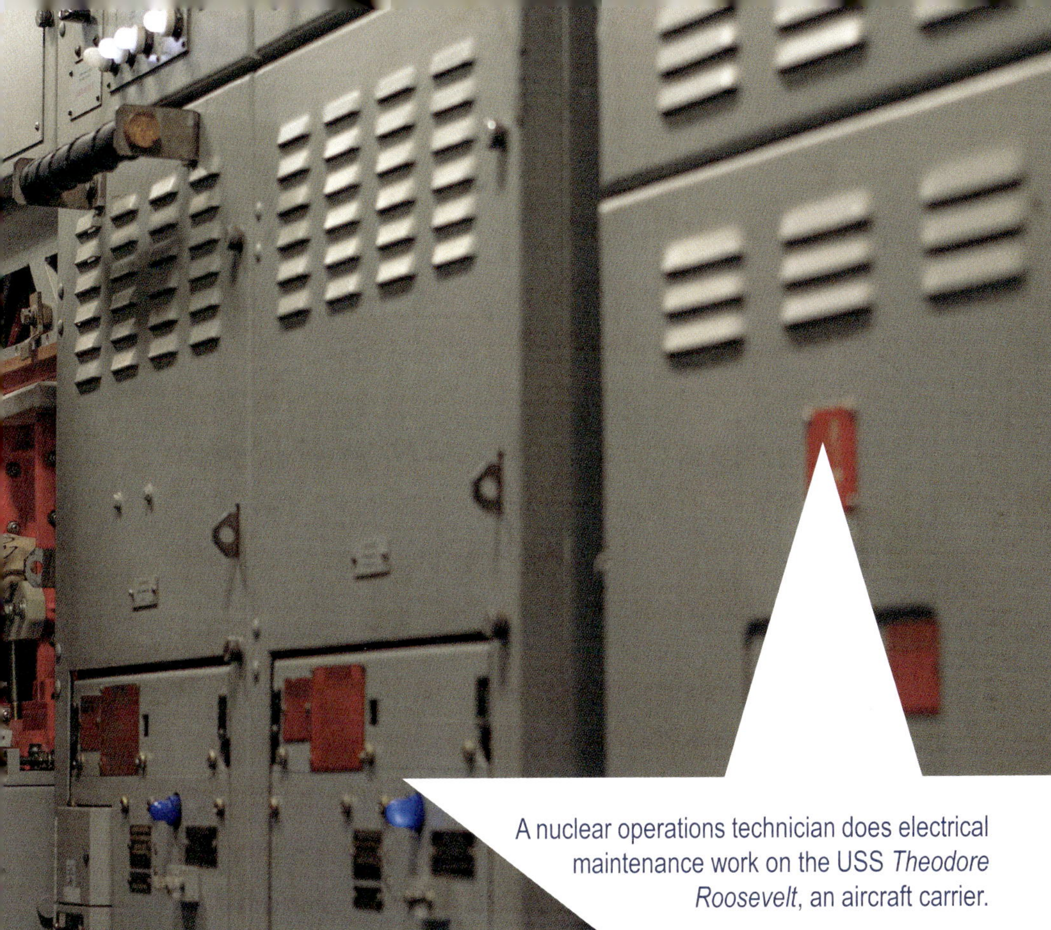

A nuclear operations technician does electrical maintenance work on the USS *Theodore Roosevelt*, an aircraft carrier.

ship or submarine through the water. It also supplies energy for all of the ship's equipment, computers, and electrical devices. When there is a problem with the plant, the ship cannot propel itself. All significant activities grind to a halt until the power is restored. Because the ship's nuclear power plant is so critical to everything it does, the officers and sailors who work in nuclear operations are essential to the ship. They constantly monitor the nuclear plant and everything on board the ship that might affect its ability to produce and supply power when needed.

ON THE JOB

Nuclear operations technicians are responsible for keeping the US Navy's nuclear-powered vessels operating smoothly. These men and women are highly trained professionals who perform everything from operating nuclear propulsion plant machinery to controlling auxiliary equipment that supports nuclear reactors. Throughout constantly changing conditions, nuclear technicians keep the plant running.

For enlisted sailors, there are three main types of nuclear operations technician jobs. A machinist mate nuclear (MMN) works in the ship's nuclear reactor room to operate and maintain the pressurized water systems and steam machinery that provide power on ships and submarines. MMNs also operate and maintain other machinery such as turbogenerators, pumps, and oil purifiers that are essential to the plant. Outside of the plant, MMNs maintain other machinery such as steering engines, elevators, refrigeration plants, air-conditioning systems, and desalinization plants.

An electrician's mate nuclear (EMN) is responsible for operating the ship's electrical power generation systems, lighting systems, electrical equipment, and electrical appliances. These crew members install and operate electrical equipment on the ship. They also inspect, test, and perform routine maintenance of electrical and electronic equipment. If needed, they repair the

NUCLEAR MARINE PROPULSION

Nuclear-powered ships rely on nuclear fission reactions that take place in the ship's nuclear reactors. A nuclear fission reaction occurs when the nucleus of an atom is split and gives off large amounts of heat and gamma radiation. The heat emitted from the nuclear reaction is used to heat water, which circulates in hollow coils surrounding the reactors. This is done at a very high pressure so the water does not boil at this point. The heated water is transferred to another set of hollow coils that has water at normal temperature, which produces enormous amounts of steam. This steam provides energy to power the ship's turbine generators, which rotate the ship's propellers and propel the ship forward. After the steam passes through the turbines, it is cooled, condensed, and recirculated. Additional power generated in this process supplies the ship with electricity.

equipment. When there is a problem with electrical power on board, EMNs are called to solve the problem.

An electronics technician nuclear (ETN) operates and performs maintenance on the electronic systems that make the ship's nuclear reactor run. On aircraft carriers and submarines, ETNs calibrate the nuclear control rods that help generate power on these ships. They operate the electronics and computer systems that safely control the ship's nuclear power plants.

Each career—MMN, EMN, and ETN—is important in making sure the navy's nuclear-powered ships and submarines run properly. "Each job is vitally important," says Master Chief Petty Officer Ronald Nagy, who works in navy nuclear operations. He explains:

WOMEN ON SUBMARINES

For decades, women were not permitted to work on navy submarines. In 2010, the navy began allowing female officers to work on submarines. Nearly a decade later, in 2017, there were approximately 80 female officers and 50 enlisted women serving in submarines.[2] The navy expects that number to increase. To accommodate female sailors, the navy is modifying existing submarines to add extra doors and specific washrooms for women. The navy is redesigning new submarines to accommodate both men and women sailors.

> *The EM's own all the associate equipment needed to generate the electricity and to move it throughout the ship. The MM's own all the equipment that moves the steam and the turbines and everything that moves the propulsion and electricity in the ship. ET's ensure they have tools to monitor the MM's systems so everything is running safely and within bounds. Without these guys, 44 percent of our fleet's combat vessels wouldn't be functional.*[1]

WORK ENVIRONMENT

Sailors in nuclear operations generally work on nuclear-powered submarines or surface ships, both at sea and on shore. They work closely with other members of the team. Because nuclear power plants on ships and subs need constant monitoring and maintenance, nuclear operations technicians often spend long hours in a ship's nuclear reactor room.

On a submarine, sailors can spend several months living and working in cramped quarters. Machinist's Mate Third Class Jonathan Ashton's first assignment after completing

★ Two nuclear machinist's mates open a throttle valve on the aircraft carrier USS *Dwight D. Eisenhower*.

Nuclear Power School was aboard the attack submarine USS *Scranton*. Ashton explains that working on a submarine can be challenging. For months at a time, the crew lives hundreds of feet below the water in a metal tube that is 33 feet (10 m) wide.[3] They are cut off from the world, with no internet, email, or social media. There are no phone lines to call family and friends with. The space is tight, and there is no sun to track when it is day or night. "You have to be a little crazy to be a submariner, but submarining runs in my blood," Ashton says as the son of a retired submariner.[4]

QUALIFICATIONS, TRAINING, AND ADVANCEMENT

Navy nuclear technicians are enlisted sailors. As such, they are required to have a high school diploma. Navy nuclear operations is a challenging, high-tech field. Candidates should have a talent for mathematics and science and must have successfully completed at least one year of algebra class in high school.

In addition, successful nuclear operations candidates are mature, responsible, and able to work well under pressure.

After completing recruit training, candidates interested in a nuclear operations job report to Class "A" School in Charleston, South Carolina, for technical training specific to their career path: MMN, EMN, or ETN. The intensive classroom-based training lasts from three to six months, depending on the specific path. Afterward, nuclear operations candidates spend six months at Naval Nuclear Power School (NNPS), also in Charleston. At NNPS, they study mathematics, physics, and basic engineering sciences. They learn the theory and practical application of nuclear physics and reactor engineering. The candidates gain a comprehensive understanding of how a naval nuclear power plant operates, including the principles of nuclear reactions,

FIREFIGHTING SKILLS

No matter what job they have, every US Navy sailor is trained to put out fires on ships and submarines. At recruit training, new recruits spend more than 40 hours training in firefighting and damage control skills so they will be ready to respond in any emergency. First, recruits learn how to use firefighting and damage control equipment. Then they practice their skills in firefighting simulations. They also conduct hands-on practice on the USS *Chief*, a controlled training environment. On the USS *Chief*, recruits test their skills while fighting real fires in shipboard compartments. As they battle the fires on the USS *Chief*, they use a variety of fire suppression agents, firefighting gear, and equipment. Firefighting skills are tested as part of recruit training's final test, Battle Stations 21.

MAKING AN IMPACT

Sailors working in nuclear operations are making an impact every day. Ships and submarines that use nuclear power have several advantages. One big benefit is that they can be at sea for months at time without needing to refuel. In addition, using nuclear power reduces the US Navy's reliance on increasingly scarce fossil fuels. But powering a vessel with nuclear power is a complex task. Without the highly trained men and women in nuclear operations, the US Navy would not be able to operate many of its ships and submarines. Nuclear operations technicians make sure that the nuclear power plants on each vessel are working safely to provide the vessel with the power it needs to move through the water and support all of the activities on board. Because of its nuclear technicians, the US Navy sails smoothly through the oceans on missions throughout the world.

how a nuclear reactor core operates, how heat and fluid transfer systems work, and how mechanical and electrical systems work.

After NNPS, candidates take the knowledge they have learned and begin hands-on training in their specialty. This rigorous training occurs at one of two Nuclear Power Training Units (NPTU), which are located in Charleston and in Ballston Spa, New York. For six months, candidates use models to practice the fundamentals of a naval nuclear power plant. They learn how the plant's mechanical, electrical, and reactor subsystems interact and work together. They also learn about nuclear radiation and safety measures to ensure the safe operation of the nuclear power plant. Upon successful completion of NPTU training, sailors are given an assignment on a nuclear-powered aircraft carrier or submarine.

In high school, Nick Reed Smith had no idea what he wanted to do with his future. After talking with a navy recruiter, he decided to enlist. He says the navy provided him with excellent training in nuclear operations. “As a nuclear machinist’s mate, I was sent to school for two years before entering the fleet. I learned a ton . . . [the program] was the most challenging thing I ever did. I worked my butt off just to stay above the failing point,” he says.[5]

There are many promotion opportunities available to sailors working in nuclear operations. Promotions are competitive and based on performance. Those who earn a bachelor’s degree, preferably in math, chemistry, physics, engineering, or a related field, are eligible to become nuclear officers on a ship or submarine. Nuclear officers oversee the sailors in the nuclear operations department. In addition, the specialized training and work experience that nuclear technicians receive can lead to opportunities in related fields.

TOP FIVE QUESTIONS

★ WHAT IS IT LIKE TO WORK IN NAVY NUCLEAR OPERATIONS?

Nuclear technicians work on nuclear-powered submarines or surface ships. They work closely with other members of the team in the ship's nuclear plant and with related equipment and systems.

★ WHAT SHOULD THOSE WHO ARE INTERESTED IN THIS CAREER STUDY IN SCHOOL?

People interested in nuclear operations careers should take classes in math, general science, physics, chemistry, and engineering.

★ WHAT SKILLS ARE BENEFICIAL FOR THOSE INTERESTED IN THIS CAREER?

Navy nuclear operations is one of the navy's most challenging technical fields. Successful candidates are good at math and science. In addition, they are able to work well in high-pressure environments and have a mature, responsible demeanor.

★ WHAT IS THE TYPICAL SALARY FOR A NUCLEAR TECHNICIAN?

In addition to receiving basic pay, sailors working in the nuclear field are eligible for enlistment bonuses.

★ AFTER THE NAVY, WHAT CIVILIAN CAREERS ARE NUCLEAR TECHNICIANS QUALIFIED FOR?

Navy-trained nuclear operations technicians are valued for their knowledge and skills in the nuclear field. After the navy, these men and women often find careers working for energy companies that operate private nuclear power plants.

CHAPTER 6

CRYPTOLOGIC TECHNICIAN

Gathering top secret intelligence is a critical part of how the military keeps the United States secure. The navy's cryptologic technicians use their skills and the latest technology to collect, decode, and translate intelligence information. They work under the oversight of information warfare officers, who

Cryptologic technicians use computers and other technology to gather and decipher intelligence information.

are highly specialized information experts, or cyber warfare engineers, who are computer experts who work to defend against cyberattacks.

CRACKING THE CODE

Cryptologic technicians collect, gather, and analyze encrypted electronic communications. They jam the enemy's radar signals, preventing it from relaying information or using radar-equipped weapons. Language experts translate communications and other information transmitted in foreign languages. Cryptologic technicians also maintain the high-tech equipment that the navy uses to gather intelligence and defend these networks from attack.

Navy cryptologic technicians usually have a specialty. Interpretive cryptologic technicians, for instance, are language experts. Their fluency in other languages allows them to interpret and translate foreign communications and information. They also provide cultural and regional guidance and expertise for service members operating in foreign countries. Other cryptologic technicians have a technical specialty. They are experts in radar signals, including airborne, shipborne, and land-based signals. They operate electronic intelligence-receiving systems, digital recording devices, and related computer equipment. They run the electronic equipment that sends high-power jamming signals to fool the enemy's electronic sensors and radar-guided weapons systems. Other cryptologic technicians

WHAT IS CRYPTOLOGY?

Cryptology is the science of secret communication. It is used by militaries, governments, and other organizations to protect valuable data and information. In order for data to be secure, it must be transformed so that it would be difficult for someone who was not supposed to see it to understand its meaning. To do this, mathematical equations are used to encrypt messages and prevent unauthorized access. The field of cryptology includes cryptography, which is the analysis of different methods used to encrypt messages, and cryptanalysis, which is the analysis of methods used to decrypt encrypted messages.

specialize in maintaining the navy's sophisticated cryptologic equipment, networks, and systems. Others specialize in intercepting and collecting enemy communication signals. Using computers and specialized electronic equipment, they analyze and report on collected signals to identify and locate potential threats.

INFORMATION DOMINANCE CORPS

Cryptologic technicians are an important part of the navy's Information Dominance Corps (IDC). Created in 2009, this group is made up of enlisted sailors, officers, and civilian professionals who specialize in information-intensive fields such as information technology, cryptology, and intelligence. They work together to develop and defend the navy's intelligence, networks, and systems and ensure the navy's technological superiority. Within the IDC, cryptologic technicians work to gather information about the enemy's operations and knowledge about the environment, conditions, and other important factors during conflicts.

Navy chief Donna Gordon is a cryptologic technician-interpretive (CTI). She uses her proficiency in languages to analyze encrypted electronic communications and decipher information in foreign languages. "Linguists aren't just interpreting and translating. We're also producing intelligence reports . . . with the potential to be seen by some high-level decision-making [personnel]," she says.[1] Gordon also provides cultural and regional guidance to US Navy personnel around the world. "The primary role of a CTI is to be that regional and cultural expert for your target language. We are considered the subject matter experts," Gordon says.[2] To stay current with her language skills, Gordon listens to foreign language music, watches foreign language television shows, and visits neighborhoods where that language is spoken.

WORK ENVIRONMENT

Cryptologic technicians can work on ships, submarines, or naval aircraft or serve at shore stations in the United States or overseas. Their work stations are generally located in clean, air-conditioned offices, computer rooms, or labs with electronic equipment. They often work for many hours a day. "I've deployed on subs which absolutely did mean spending 12 hours in a dark room either translating or listening to white noise," says one ten-year CTI veteran.[3]

Sometimes, cryptologic technicians serve with overseas units. A cryptologic technician-collection (CTR) described her experience hunting pirates off the coast of Africa in a US Navy recruitment video online. "We were hanging out off the coast of Somalia for two and a half months hunting pirates. The piracy operations included monitoring some shorter wave communications, and then when we would come to a pirate [ship], our search-and-rescue team would board those vessels," she says.[4]

★ Cryptologic technicians often spend a lot of time working in computer labs.

QUALIFICATIONS AND EDUCATION

Cryptologic technicians are enlisted sailors and need to have a high school diploma. To prepare for this career, high school students should take classes in computer and network technology, computer programming, and math. Students interested in the language specialty should also study foreign languages and cultures.

Because they handle classified information and communications, cryptologic technicians must have Top Secret/ Sensitive Compartmented Information security clearances, which allow them access to classified information or restricted areas after the completion of a thorough background check. In order to gain these security clearances, candidates must be US citizens who do not have criminal records. They must also pass a background investigation, with a reinvestigation every five years to maintain the security clearance. People who have been convicted of drug charges are typically ineligible for this career.

EARNING CERTIFICATIONS

For many navy careers, earning certifications demonstrates that a sailor has mastered certain skills. This can make them more likely to be promoted. For cryptologic technicians, there are many navy-funded certifications available, including those in networking, network security, computer forensics, and language skills. Those trained in network specialties can earn certifications in computer hardware and architecture, networking concepts and design, protocol analysis, Windows and Unix programming, and network defense and forensics. In addition, the specialized training that navy cryptologic technicians receive can help them obtain civilian certifications from a number of national boards and organizations.

To become a cryptologic technician, candidates must meet the navy's physical standards for fitness, weight, and/or percentage of body fat. They must also have normal hearing. Candidates for technical and maintenance specialties must have normal color perception.

Cryptologic technicians should have a good understanding of computers, electrical and mechanical systems, satellite systems, and other high-tech equipment. They should have the ability to understand and apply math concepts. They should also be able to speak and write well and communicate effectively. Cryptologic technicians need to be able to think creatively, solve problems, and adapt to changing conditions.

Cryptologic technicians often work as part of a team. Therefore, the ability to work well with others is an important trait for people considering this career. Also, cryptologic technicians should be able to take and follow orders from superior officers. When stress levels are high during a military operation, they should be able to operate calmly and efficiently.

TRAINING AND ADVANCEMENT

After basic training, cryptologic technician candidates receive specific training at Class "A" School in either Pensacola, Florida, or Monterey, California, to prepare for their specific careers as navy cryptologic technicians. This training develops the working

MAKING AN IMPACT

What the US military does not know can hurt the country. That is why the US Navy gathers intelligence all the time, every day. Using language, analytical, and technical skills, navy personnel decipher communications signals and decode recordings. They conduct radar surveillance and jam guided weapons systems. As the world becomes more connected online, protecting digital computers, systems, and networks is essential. Every day, navy cryptologic technicians work to maintain US cybersecurity. They are an essential part of gathering top secret intelligence to keep the United States and its citizens safe.

★ Part of cryptologic technician training includes classroom instruction.

knowledge the sailors will need for their first assignments on a ship or at a shore station. Training includes classroom lectures as well as hands-on instruction with equipment. It includes extensive technical preparation in computer systems, network configuration, communication techniques and platforms, cryptographic equipment operations, and security policies and procedures. Candidates pursuing a language specialty receive comprehensive foreign language instruction. After "A" school, some cryptologic technicians attend advanced training specific to their specialty.

As cryptologic technicians advance to higher ranks, they take on more supervisory and administrative roles. Earning certifications can also make cryptologic technicians eligible for promotions. Navy personnel in this field who earn a bachelor's degree may advance to become foreign area officers. These officers provide operational experience, language expertise, and cultural knowledge to other navy personnel.

TOP FIVE QUESTIONS

WHAT IS IT LIKE TO WORK AS A CRYPTOLOGIC TECHNICIAN?

Cryptologic technicians use specialized equipment to collect, gather, and analyze encrypted electronic communications. Some are language experts who translate decrypted communications and other information. Cryptologic technicians also operate equipment that can prevent enemies from sending radar messages or using radar-equipped weapons.

WHAT SHOULD STUDENTS INTERESTED IN THIS CAREER STUDY IN SCHOOL?

Classes in math, computer programming, and computer and network technology are relevant to the cryptologic technician career. Those interested in becoming language specialists should also study foreign languages and cultures.

WHAT SKILLS ARE BENEFICIAL TO THIS CAREER?

It is helpful for cryptologic technicians to have a good understanding of computers, satellite systems, and other high-tech equipment. They should also have strong math skills and be able to communicate clearly. In addition, cryptologic technicians should be able to think creatively, solve problems, and adapt to changing conditions.

WHAT IS THE TYPICAL SALARY FOR THIS CAREER?

Along with the basic pay provided to all navy personnel, sailors working in some cryptologic technician specialties are also eligible for enlistment bonuses.

AFTER THE NAVY, WHAT CIVILIAN CAREERS ARE CRYPTOLOGIC TECHNICIANS QUALIFIED FOR?

Navy cryptologic technicians have specialized training, expertise, and security clearances that may allow them to work in jobs with the federal government, including jobs in intelligence and information technology management. In addition, they can work for companies in various computer specialties or as radio, cellular, and network equipment installers and repairers.

CHAPTER 7

NAVY NURSE

Nurses provide treatment for thousands of US Navy sailors, their families, and people in need worldwide. Navy nurses provide routine, preventative, and emergency care just like nurses in traditional hospitals and medical offices. Often, navy nurses provide care in nontraditional settings, such as on hospital ships or aircraft carriers.

US Navy nurses provide medical care to people all over the world.

ON THE JOB

Navy nurses work closely with navy physicians, surgeons, and other health professionals to care for patients. They provide care and treatment for sick and injured navy sailors and their families. On any given day, they change bandages and administer medications. They measure and monitor patients' vital signs and record patient information in medical charts. Some navy nurses also write prescriptions. Others are responsible for training navy hospital corpsmen, who are enlisted medical specialists who assist navy physicians and nurses in providing medical care.

Sometimes, navy nurses and other health professionals provide emergency medical care in developing countries or on the battlefield. They take part in humanitarian relief efforts such as vaccinating infants in developing countries or providing emergency care to people injured in natural disasters. While in the field, navy nurses perform triage to assess patients to determine the severity of their injuries and decide how they should be treated.

Navy nurses often specialize in a certain area of nursing care. Some may work in a critical care unit, while others provide care in an emergency room. Other nursing specialties include surgical care, psychiatric care, and child health care.

After graduating from college in 2017, Ensign Allison O'Neill was commissioned into the US Navy Nurse Corps. After passing her registered nurse licensing exam, she reported for her first assignment at the US Naval Hospital in Okinawa, Japan. O'Neill spent the next eight weeks in a residency for new nurses, in which she rotated through almost every unit in the hospital. After completing the residency, she was assigned to the hospital's mother-infant care center for labor and delivery. O'Neill's unit is one of the busiest in the hospital, averaging 250 triage visits per month and 100 deliveries per month.[1] She says working with patients and staff every day has given her a wealth of experience. Because many of the navy patients she treats are American, O'Neill says it can be easy to forget that she is living across the world in another country. To take advantage of the opportunity, she says, "I made a concerted effort to start exploring this community, culture and area of the world right away."[2] For others considering a career as a navy nurse working overseas, O'Neill suggests brushing up on language skills. "If you didn't study it before coming, there are numerous ways to learn once there. You can buy books, use apps . . . find an online tutor or, most simply, meet people! I joined a local language [group] that gathers once a week to practice conversation," she says.[3]

USNS *COMFORT*

The USNS *Comfort* is one of the US Navy's two hospital ships. A converted oil supertanker, the *Comfort* has provided aid to people in need since 1987. The ship has 12 operating rooms and 1,000 beds for patients.[4] The ship also houses a dental clinic, an optometry lab, four X-ray machines, and a CT scanner. The ship has a medical supply depot and a stocked pharmacy, too. The *Comfort* has been deployed during conflicts such as the Persian Gulf War (1990–1991) and the Iraq War (2003–2011). It also sailed to provide natural disaster relief during Hurricane Katrina in 2005 and Hurricane Maria in 2017. In 2019, the *Comfort* was deployed on a five-month humanitarian mission to the Caribbean, Central America, and South America to support local medical systems that were being overwhelmed by an increase in refugees.

FLIGHT NURSE

Navy flight nurses receive specialized training so they can evacuate patients and care for them in flight. Lieutenant Commander Kimberly Albero served as a navy flight nurse with the First Medical Battalion supporting the US Marines during Operation Enduring Freedom in Afghanistan. Albero was sent to a forward operating base as a critical care nurse attached to the shock trauma platoon. She worked as an intensive care nurse on a surgical team along with four surgeons, two anesthesiologists, one emergency room nurse, and one medical-surgical nurse. Albero flew with wounded marines and coalition soldiers from where they were injured to the British trauma hospital at Camp Bastion, a British air base in Afghanistan. At Camp Bastion, wounded soldiers received lifesaving care and surgery before being transported home to the United States. After her deployment, Albero returned to work as an ICU nurse at the naval hospital in San Diego, California. She says her time as a flight nurse was one of the most fulfilling experiences of her life.

WORK ENVIRONMENT

There are more than 250 US Navy medical facilities around the world where navy nurses may work.[5] Navy nurses typically work indoors at hospitals or clinics with other medical staff. Some nurses work on hospital ships or large warships. While they often work as part of a team, some may work individually at times.

Navy nurses can also work in the field. They may be attached to a field unit supporting navy and marine forces in combat zones. When a natural disaster strikes, navy nurses may be deployed to help provide emergency aid to civilians. Some navy nurses provide care on aircraft while transporting patients to hospitals.

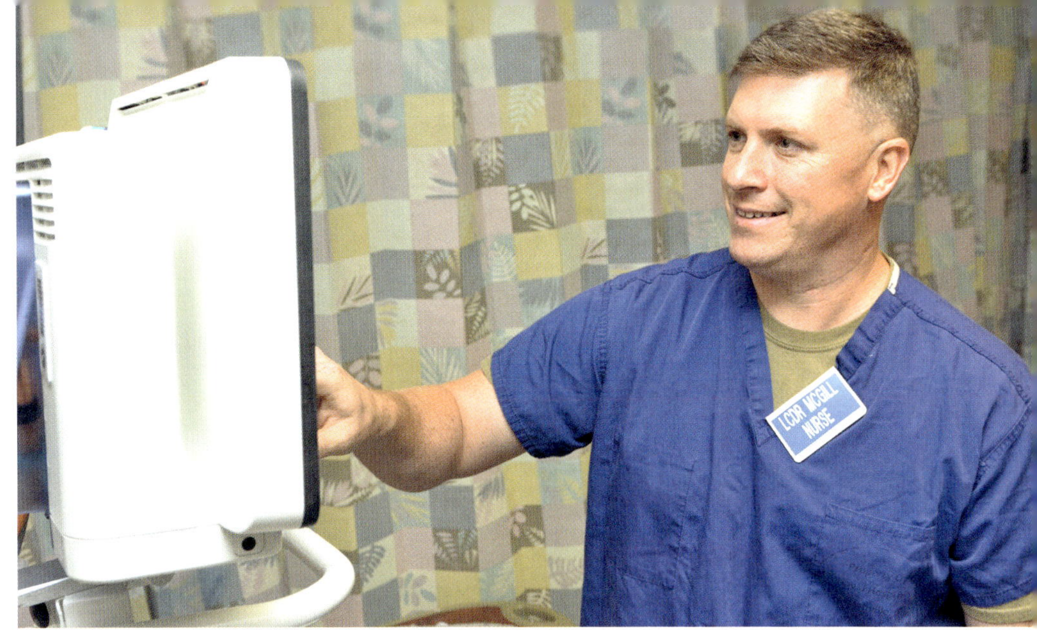

★ A navy nurse checks a patient's monitor at Naval Hospital Jacksonville in Florida.

Navy hospitals and medical facilities provide skilled care 24 hours a day, seven days a week. While some navy nurses work regular hours in a hospital, others may work long shifts or in dangerous locations close to combat. According to Rear Admiral Tina Davidson, a director in the US Navy Nurse Corps, there is no typical day for a navy nurse. She says:

> *That is what's so great about being a navy nurse. Navy nurses are versatile and care for our warfighters and their families in a multitude of environments, from shipboard, to the field with marines, as flight nurses, to serving in academic positions teaching corpsmen as well as other nurses. We also have nurses in staff jobs and executive medicine. Regardless of where we serve, we are leaders at every level and committed to lifelong learning.*[6]

EDUCATION

Navy nurses are commissioned officers. They are required to have a bachelor of science degree from an accredited nursing program at a four-year college or university. They must also have a license to practice as a registered nurse in a US state or territory or in Washington, DC. Navy nurses have one year after starting active duty to obtain their nursing license.

Navy nurses attend Officer Development School (ODS) in Newport, Rhode Island. This five-week program provides an intense, comprehensive introduction to the responsibilities of navy staff corps officers. Staff corps officers are commissioned officers in careers that also exist outside of the military. They work as physicians, lawyers, chaplains, and nurses.

PAYING FOR NURSING SCHOOL

The navy requires its nurses to obtain their college degrees from accredited nursing programs. For some navy nurse candidates, this can be a financial hardship. The navy offers several ways to help students pay for nursing school. Some high school students choose to join the Naval Reserve Officers Training Corps (NROTC). Under the Nurse Option scholarship, the navy can cover up to $180,000 for nursing education at colleges and universities across the country. Students can focus on their nursing education with no military obligation until they graduate. Alternatively, under the Nurse Candidate Program, nursing students can receive an initial grant and a monthly stipend for up to 24 months to help pay for nursing school. Either option can help students who are interested in becoming navy nurses get the education they need.

MAKING AN IMPACT

Navy nurses provide medical treatment and help save lives. As a member of the US Navy Nurse Corps, Lieutenant Logan Moore is a trauma and en route care nurse assigned to Naval Amphibious Forces. He provides critical care to patients during crisis response missions. He is proud of being able to make a difference in the lives of others. "I feel like I am making a difference every time the team goes from one place to another to support a mission," Moore said.[7]

ODS includes instruction about the military structure of the US Navy and its history, traditions, and customs. It also includes leadership development and military etiquette instruction.

After ODS, navy nurses are assigned to their first duty either at a navy medical treatment facility or on board a navy vessel. There, they receive further experience and training on the job. After their first duty assignment, navy nurses are eligible for promotions, which are competitive and based on performance.

PHYSICAL REQUIREMENTS

Navy nurses must be between the ages of 18 and 31 when they join the navy. They must also be US citizens and must be willing to serve a minimum of three years of active duty service. Every navy sailor, including navy nurses, must pass a physical fitness test, which includes pull-ups, sit-ups, a 1.5-mile (2.4 km) run, and a 400- or 500-yard (366 or 457 m) swim. Working as a navy nurse can be physically demanding, as nurses have to lift and carry patients and medical equipment. Therefore, nurses should have the physical strength and stamina to handle these tasks.

Nurses must also pass a full medical examination. They are not required to have 20/20 vision, but they must meet certain height and weight requirements.

SKILLS AND PERSONALITY

Generally, the work of navy nurses involves serving others and requires good judgment, mental alertness, and the ability to be calm under stress. Nurses should enjoy working with people and have excellent interpersonal skills, as they will be interacting with patients and other medical staff on a regular basis. Having a caring bedside manner can help make patients feel more comfortable. Navy nurses often have to communicate information about a patient's condition or explain discharge instructions. To be effective, they should be able to speak and write well and communicate clearly. Other important skills for this career include the ability to perform detailed and repetitive work and keep accurate records.

While navy nurses must commit to three years of active duty, many stay much longer. Davidson initially planned to complete her three-year commitment and then return to civilian nursing. "It didn't take long for me to realize what an honor and privilege it was to care for America's warfighters and their families," she says. "Three years turned into more than 30 years and now I have so many fond memories of my time in the navy. I can't imagine a different career."[8]

TOP FIVE QUESTIONS

★ WHAT IS IT LIKE TO WORK AS A NAVY NURSE?

Just like nurses in traditional hospitals, navy nurses provide routine care, preventative care, and emergency care. They do this for sailors and their families, as well as for others in need around the world. In addition to working in hospitals and medical offices, navy nurses provide care on hospital ships and aircraft carriers.

★ WHAT SHOULD PEOPLE WHO ARE INTERESTED IN THIS CAREER STUDY IN SCHOOL?

Classes in mathematics, biology, chemistry, anatomy, and other general sciences are helpful to people interested in becoming navy nurses. These students should also consider taking courses in emergency medicine and cardiopulmonary resuscitation (CPR).

★ WHAT SKILLS ARE BENEFICIAL FOR THOSE INTERESTED IN THIS CAREER?

Good communication skills and a caring personality are helpful to navy nurses. Nurses should also be able to remain calm under stress.

★ WHAT IS THE TYPICAL SALARY FOR A NAVY NURSE?

As of January 2019, the base salary for active duty commissioned officers in the navy, which include nurses, started at $38,268 for officers with less than two years of service.[9]

★ AFTER THE NAVY, WHAT CIVILIAN CAREERS ARE NAVY NURSES QUALIFIED FOR?

Nurses who leave the navy often work in civilian hospitals, medical centers, and physician's offices in a variety of roles and specialties.

CHAPTER 8

EXPLOSIVE ORDNANCE DISPOSAL TECHNICIAN

When dangerous explosives threaten the safety of navy sailors and civilians, explosive ordnance disposal (EOD) technicians respond. Always ready, EOD technicians render any type of explosive ordnance, or explosive weapon, safe. They investigate and demolish natural and man-made underwater

An EOD technician makes sure the entrance to a building is safe.

obstructions. They safely handle chemical, biological, and nuclear weapons. EODs also prepare coastal regions for amphibious landings. Whether wearing bomb suits or using high-tech robotic technology, navy EODs use their skills to keep others safe.

WORKING AS AN EOD

Navy EODs work on missions around the world. They locate and identify all forms of explosives, including those on land and underwater. Underwater, they locate and neutralize sea mines, torpedoes, and depth charge explosives to keep the navy fleet safe. They render an ordnance safe by safely triggering or burning it. To reach explosives in difficult locations, navy EODs are experts in diving and parachuting and are trained to work under enemy fire, just as combat soldiers are.

EOD technicians are often called to support special operations forces such as the Navy SEALs and the Army Special Forces. In addition to working closely with other military branches and special forces, navy EOD technicians are sometimes asked to support civilian law enforcement agencies.

The work of an EOD technician is often difficult and dangerous. In October 2016, while clearing an area of explosive hazards, Explosive Ordnance Disposal Technician First Class Jeffrey Thomas found himself and his convoy in the midst of a firefight with the Islamic State of Iraq and Syria (ISIS). Throughout the firefight, Thomas and his team in the Explosive Ordnance Disposal Mobile Unit 3 constantly dodged small arms fire, rocket-propelled grenades, and mortar fire to clear a path for the US military convoy. When the lead vehicle rolled over an improvised explosive device (IED) that killed Thomas's EOD supervisor, Thomas got out of his vehicle and swept the rest of the area for explosives despite the enemy fire all around him. Thomas cleared a path to allow medics to reach and evacuate casualties. With the enemy still firing on them, Thomas guided

WOMEN EOD TECHNICIANS

The first female EOD technicians graduated from the Naval School Explosive Ordnance Disposal in 1980. Today, women make up approximately 2 percent of the overall navy EOD force. Ensign Brie Coger is an EOD officer at EOD Mobile Unit One in San Diego, California. She says she wanted to become an EOD technician because of the challenge it presents both physically and mentally. Although she has not yet been in combat, Coger has honed her skills on many assignments such as working and training with other EOD technicians from countries around the world.[2]

the convoy out of the minefield to a medical evacuation landing zone. For his bravery that day, Thomas was awarded the Silver Star, the military's third-highest award for valor. "Jeff knowingly exposed himself to hazards in order to protect the lives of his teammates and brothers in arms, and secure a [medical evacuation] for his wounded teammate. His actions that day saved the lives of his teammates and exceeded all measures of selflessness and devotion to his country," said Commander Geoff Townsend, the commanding officer of Thomas's unit.[1]

WORK ENVIRONMENT

Navy EODs work anywhere in the world. They may perform tasks at remote locations, on aircraft carriers, or at military stations. Their missions take them to all environments and every climate around the world. They may work in the water or on land.

EOD technicians typically work in five- to 12-person teams. How they get to where they are needed depends on the type of mission, the unit they are supporting, weather conditions, and the required equipment for the mission. Sometimes they ride a diving rig and scuba dive deep under the water. Other times, they parachute from an aircraft or helicopter. In other situations, EODs ride in small boats or tracked vehicles to reach their mission.

QUALIFICATIONS, TRAINING, AND ADVANCEMENT

Navy EOD technicians are enlisted sailors, so they are required to have their high school diplomas. Candidates for this job must also be 30 years old or younger. The job of a navy EOD technician is physically challenging. Besides being in top physical condition, people who wish to become navy EOD technicians must have normal color vision and have uncorrected vision that is no worse than 20/200 and correctable to 20/25. EOD technicians must pass the navy's physical fitness test. They must also pass a hyperbaric pressure tolerance test to make sure their bodies can handle deep-sea diving. An enlisted EOD technician with a bachelor's degree can eventually be promoted to become an EOD officer.

EOD technician candidates must endure 51 weeks of grueling training that challenges them both mentally and physically. After completing basic recruit training, EOD candidates attend a three-week EOD Prep Course in Great Lakes, Illinois. In this

★ EOD technicians sometimes work with remote-controlled robots to safely neutralize explosive devices.

course, recruits practice swim stroke development, long-range swimming skills, and physical conditioning.

Afterward, recruits move on to Dive School at the Naval Diving and Salvage Training Center (NDSTC) in Panama City, Florida. In this nine-week course, they receive training in a variety of areas including scuba diving, dive physics, physiology, and basic dive medicine. Recruits also train on equipment such as the MK16 underwater rebreather. A rebreather is a closed circuit that cleans out carbon dioxide from the diver's exhalations and adds oxygen back in for inhalation. This creates no bubbles, which is critical when disarming an underwater mine. "You know whenever you scuba dive, the bubbles 'wump wump wump,' they make an acoustic signature, which can set off the underwater ordnance. So, you don't want that if you're disarming underwater

★ A group of navy EOD technicians lowers a robot into the water. They can control the robot remotely to locate threats.

ordnance," explains Matt Lutz, a former navy EOD technician and combat veteran who served in Iraq and Afghanistan.[3]

After completing Dive School, candidates attend Naval School Explosive Ordnance Disposal at Eglin Air Force Base in Fort Walton Beach, Florida. For the next 42 weeks, recruits learn how to render safe or defuse different types of ordnance. Training is divided into four main categories. The Air Ordnance Division focuses on bombs and missiles. The Nuclear Ordnance Division trains recruits in basic nuclear physics, radiation monitoring, and safe decontamination procedures. The Underwater Ordnance Division trains recruits in how to handle torpedoes and other types of underwater explosives. It also teaches various underwater search procedures. A fourth category trains recruits to handle IEDs, including homemade bombs.

After finishing basic EOD school, recruits attend Basic Airborne Training (also known as Jump School) at Fort Benning, Georgia, where they qualify as basic parachutists. The final step is EOD Tactical Training in San Diego, California. In this

MAKING AN IMPACT

EOD technicians are in constant demand to disable and destroy the improvised bombs and other explosives used by various insurgent forces around the world. Working in one of the most dangerous jobs in the navy, these brave men and women are responsible for saving many lives and keeping troops safe. Explosive Ordnance Disposal Technician First Class Brian Oberley is an example of how EOD technicians make a difference in the lives of others. While assigned to Special Forces Operation Detachment Alpha in 2017, he supported 65 combat patrols with his in-depth knowledge of enemy IEDs. With his help, the patrols were able to safely dispose of 900 pounds (408 kg) of unexploded ordnance. He also led an operation to find and safely dispose of six explosives that were a serious threat to US forces and everyone in the area. As recognition for his work, Oberley received a Bronze Star Medal.[4]

JUMP SCHOOL

At the Army's Basic Airborne Course, or Jump School, members of different branches of the military, including the navy, learn how to jump out of an aircraft, navigate using a parachute, and land safely on the ground. In the demanding three-week training, candidates spend the first week learning how to land safely. They gradually practice jumps from a 34-foot (10 m) tower. In the second week, candidates practice jumping from the 34-foot (10 m) tower using different harnesses and equipment. By the end of the week, they complete a parachute jump off a 250-foot (76 m) tower. During the third week, candidates practice their skills jumping out of aircraft in flight. Each candidate must complete five jumps, including a night jump, to graduate from Jump School.

three-week course, recruits learn the basics of how to drop into an area from a helicopter and how to use various guns and other weapons. They also learn basic small unit tactics and how to communicate in dangerous situations.

Once recruits successfully complete all EOD training, they are assigned to an EOD Mobile Unit. There, they gain advanced on-the-job training and experience. "We have one of the longest training pipelines in the military, especially with navy EOD because we go through a lot more training than the other branches," Lutz says.[5]

TOP FIVE QUESTIONS

★ WHAT IS IT LIKE TO WORK AS AN EOD TECHNICIAN?

EOD technicians have one of the most dangerous jobs in the navy. They save others by disarming and defusing explosive devices, on land and underwater.

★ WHAT SHOULD THOSE WHO ARE INTERESTED IN THIS CAREER STUDY IN SCHOOL?

Students interested in becoming EOD technicians should take physical education classes in high school to get in top shape before joining the navy. They should also take English, mathematics, and basic sciences courses to prepare for the ASVAB test.

★ WHAT SKILLS ARE BENEFICIAL FOR THOSE INTERESTED IN THIS CAREER?

EOD technician candidates should be in top physical condition. Because they often work in high-stress and high-pressure situations to find and disarm deadly explosives, they should be able to stay calm and focused in difficult conditions. In addition, EOD technicians should have a good eye for detail, which can help them find and identify hidden dangers.

★ WHAT IS THE TYPICAL SALARY FOR AN EOD TECHNICIAN?

In addition to basic pay, EOD technicians are eligible for enlistment bonuses and special duty assignment pay. In January 2019, the base salary for active duty enlisted service members, which include EOD technicians, started at $20,172 (less than two years of service).[6]

★ WHAT CIVILIAN CAREERS ARE EOD TECHNICIANS QUALIFIED FOR AFTER THEY LEAVE THE NAVY?

After the navy, EOD technicians often work for law enforcement agencies, such as the Federal Bureau of Investigation (FBI), Transportation Security Administration (TSA), or local police and fire departments. Additionally, some EOD technicians work for companies that send teams of EOD specialists around the world to find and safely explode and dispose of all types of explosives.

CHAPTER 9

SONAR TECHNICIAN

Sonar technicians are the underwater eyes and ears of the US Navy. They use advanced sonar technology to conduct underwater surveillance and help the fleet navigate and conduct search-and-rescue operations. Navy sonar technicians detect, identify, and track other ships or submarines in the water. They use this information to keep navy vessels safe at sea.

Sonar technicians use high-tech equipment to monitor everything that is happening underwater around the navy's ships.

ON THE JOB

Navy sonar technicians have a critical role in navigation at sea. They operate all different types of sonar systems and oceanographic equipment on cruisers, destroyers, and submarines. They are highly trained in electronics and acoustics on ships and submarines. They use sonar sensors to find and identify objects underwater. They also operate underwater fire control systems, which assist a weapon system in targeting, tracking, and striking its target.

When a sonar system picks up any type of underwater sound, sonar technicians work to identify it. The sound could be made by surface ships, torpedoes, submarines, jamming technologies, or other sonar transmissions. It could also come from marine life. Sonar technicians use highly specialized equipment such as bathythermographs, which detect changes in water temperature versus depth, and fathometers, which use sound waves to measure depth. Once they have collected sonar data, sonar technicians analyze and interpret it. They prepare and update charts and plots. Sonar technicians are also responsible for repairing sonar systems.

On submarines, sonar technicians are responsible for the sub's navigation. They also serve as the sub's oceanographers and evaluate anything in the sea that affects the sub's ability to move. Seaman Apprentice Preston Speicher is a member of a submarine force that patrols under the water's surface. Speicher is stationed

ACTIVE SONAR

Sonar, which stands for *sound navigation and ranging*, uses sound waves to detect objects on or under the surface of the water. In water, sound waves travel farther than radar and light waves. Active sonar emits pulses of sound into the water, while passive sonar listens to sounds in the ocean without emitting a signal. If there is an object in the path of the active sonar sound wave, it bounces off the object and returns an echo to the sonar system. The sonar system can then measure the strength of the signal. By measuring the time between the emission of the sound pulse and its return, the sonar system can calculate the location and position of the object in the water.

PASSIVE SONAR

Unlike active sonar systems that emit sound waves to detect objects in the water, passive sonar systems detect noise from marine objects such as submarines, ships, and marine animals. Passive sonar does not emit a signal. Instead, it quietly listens to sounds in the ocean and detects sound waves coming toward it. Alone, a single passive sonar device cannot measure how far away an object is. However, several passive sonar devices working together can determine the location of a sound source.

at the Naval Submarine Base Kings Bay in Georgia and works as a submarine sonar technician. He is assigned to the USS *Maryland*, a ballistic missile submarine. "As a sonar technician, my main goal is to listen to different sound waves to keep the ship safe for navigation," Speicher says.[1] Speicher is part of one of two rotating crews. Having two crews allows the submarine to be regularly deployed on missions without exhausting one crew. On average, submarines like the USS *Maryland* spend 77 days at sea before returning to port for 35 days of maintenance.[2]

WORK ENVIRONMENT

Some sonar technicians work on surface ships, while others work on submarines. Sonar technicians typically work in computer equipment rooms. They work closely with other sailors. They often spend a lot of time away from home, stationed on vessels in remote locations.

★ Sonar technicians must work well with each other and other sailors.

Spending so much time together helps sailors bond with each other. Master Chief Petty Officer Billy Singletary is a sonar technician on the USS *John Warner*, a fast-attack submarine based in Norfolk, Virginia. "It's like an extended family living aboard," Singletary says. "You get to know everyone on a first-name basis, and you get involved with their personal lives."[3]

On ships and submarines, sonar technicians travel all over the world. During an overseas deployment in 2018, the USS *John Warner* engaged in combat operations and launched Tomahawk cruise missiles in targeted strikes against Syrian military facilities. The sub sailed more than 30,000 nautical miles (55,560 km).[4] The sub's crew members visited ports in Greece, Spain, and the United Kingdom, and they sailed above the Arctic Circle.

On a submarine, living and working quarters can be tight. Petty Officer First Class Timothy Mays, a sonar technician on a navy submarine, explains:

> *When you are in the submarine force, you're at sea more often than not. You have no personal external communication with the outside world for extended periods, and you can't see the sun or anything else. All you have is a steel tube with machinery and 130 or more people onboard. You learn how to live with a lot of different people in close proximity. It's a skill set you develop, the ability to work together in a small, confined enclosure for very long periods of time with the same group of people under high levels of stress.*[5]

LIVING QUARTERS IN THE NAVY

When stationed at a navy base on shore, sailors typically have three living options: barracks (which is like a college dorm), an apartment, or a house. Navy housing typically provides access to full kitchens, recreational areas, laundry, and gyms. Sailors with families can live in navy houses on base, which often have three or four bedrooms, a garage, a porch, and a yard. While at sea, sailors' living quarters have an area where they can store personal items and an assigned rack for sleeping. In the galley (kitchen), cooks prepare food for the crew. On mess decks, sailors participate in recreation activities and eat meals. In crew lounges, they can watch television or play games when not on duty. Many ships have ATMs, internet access, and postal services so sailors can keep in touch with family and friends.

EDUCATION AND TRAINING

Navy sonar technicians are enlisted sailors. In addition to having a high school diploma, navy sonar technicians must also be US citizens between the ages of 17 and 34. They must have normal color vision and average to above-average hearing. They must be able to speak clearly and have good manual dexterity. Successful sonar technicians know how to pay attention to detail.

After completing recruit training, surface ship sonar technicians complete a six-week basic electronics course at the Great Lakes Naval Training Center in Illinois. Then they head to the Naval Training Center in San Diego, California, for ten weeks of Class "A" School, where they learn the basics of how to operate and maintain sonar systems and underwater surveillance equipment. They also learn how to use the ship's electronic systems and data collection equipment.

Submarine sonar technicians train for nine weeks at Basic Enlisted Submarine School in Groton, Connecticut. The course teaches the new recruit the basics of submarine systems. Upon completion, candidates go to Class "A" Technical School at the Naval Submarine Base New London in Groton, Connecticut. During this 37-week school, candidates study electricity, electronics, and computer technical skills in depth. They also learn underwater surveillance techniques and how to collect scientific data.

After completing "A" school, both surface and submarine sonar technicians begin intense on-the-job training on the specific type of navy vessel they will be assigned to. "When I went through advanced training," Mays says, "I was taught the basics of sound and how it works in water, how things move in the water and how to calculate the geometries. After you're assigned to your submarine, you learn a lot of the technical details of your system."[6]

A REWARDING CAREER

A career in the US Navy is not a good fit for everyone. It is very controlled, with service members being expected to follow rules, obey orders, and meet intensive physical fitness standards.

MAKING AN IMPACT

On any navy ship, sonar technicians are critical to the safety of the vessel and its crew. They are the eyes and ears of the ship, keeping watch and identifying objects in the water. They use this information to help vessels navigate and avoid obstacles on the surface and underwater. In times of conflict, sonar technicians use sophisticated systems to track and identify enemy ships and submarines before the enemy can launch a surprise attack. Without sonar technicians, the navy's ships and submarines would be sailing blind in dangerous seas.

★ US Navy personnel work in many different jobs at sea, all around the world.

Yet for many people, a navy career can be very rewarding. Navy personnel travel the world, working in many locations on land and at sea. They receive intense training with state-of-the-art equipment that prepares them for navy careers and future careers in the civilian world. Service members can pursue their interests and choose from many career fields. Because of the many opportunities in the navy, people of all different backgrounds and interests can find a navy career that is the perfect fit.

★ TOP FIVE QUESTIONS

★ WHAT IS IT LIKE TO WORK AS A SONAR TECHNICIAN?

Sonar technicians use advanced sonar technology to conduct underwater surveillance and help the ship or submarine navigate the ocean. They frequently spend long hours on a ship or submarine, often in remote locations.

★ WHAT SHOULD THOSE WHO ARE INTERESTED IN THIS CAREER STUDY IN SCHOOL?

People who want to become sonar technicians should take math, science, and computer technology classes in school. Any experience working with electronics would also be beneficial.

★ WHAT SKILLS ARE BENEFICIAL FOR THOSE INTERESTED IN THIS CAREER?

Sonar technicians should have superior attention to detail and good manual dexterity. They should be able to spend long hours in front of computer screens to monitor for unknown objects in the water.

★ WHAT IS THE TYPICAL SALARY FOR A SONAR TECHNICIAN?

In the navy, basic pay is based on a service member's rank and years of service. As of January 2019, the base salary for active duty enlisted service members, which include sonar technicians, started at $20,172 (less than two years of service).[7] Sonar technicians, like other military personnel, also receive various allowances such as money to pay for housing.

★ WHAT CIVILIAN CAREERS ARE SONAR TECHNICIANS QUALIFIED FOR AFTER SERVING IN THE NAVY?

After the navy, sonar technicians can use their skills and training for careers in meteorology, computer science, or electronics and mechanical work.

ESSENTIAL FACTS

US NAVY HISTORY

- 1775: General George Washington urges the Continental Congress to form a national navy.
- 1794: Congress votes to reestablish a national navy and authorizes the construction of six new vessels.
- 1861: The American Civil War begins and both the North and South start shipbuilding programs.
- 1918: After World War I, aviation becomes increasingly important to naval operations.
- 1941: Japan attacks the Pearl Harbor naval base in Hawaii. The US Navy suffers heavy losses, and the United States enters World War II.
- 1944: The US Navy provides essential ships for the D-day landings on France's Normandy beaches during World War II.
- 1954: The USS *Nautilus*, the first nuclear-powered submarine, launches.
- 1960: The USS *Enterprise*, the US Navy's first nuclear-powered aircraft carrier, launches.
- 1991: The US Navy participates with other forces in the Persian Gulf War.
- 2000s: The US Navy provides bases for air operations during invasions of Afghanistan and Iraq.

US NAVY ORGANIZATION

The US Navy is organized into two main branches: operating forces and shore establishment. The navy's operating forces branch is responsible for carrying out naval missions and exercises. It is divided into nine commands, which are further divided into numbered fleets. Each numbered fleet operates in a specific geographic area with a number of ships, submarines, and aircraft. The number of active fleets can vary from year to year. As of 2019, the US Navy had seven active fleets. The US Navy's administrative branch is the shore establishment.

CAREER MOVES

How can you prepare for a career in the US Navy?

- ★ Take English, math, science, and engineering classes to prepare for the ASVAB test, which all military recruits must take.
- ★ Get into good physical shape through running or other cardiovascular exercise, weight training, and flexibility training.
- ★ Practice swimming skills.
- ★ If possible, take water-rescue training classes or CPR training.
- ★ Talk to recruiters or other US Navy personnel about what to expect in the navy.

IMPACT ON SOCIETY

Since its formation, the US Navy has defended the waters and protected the United States, its citizens, and its allies. To do this, the US Navy trains, maintains, and equips the country's naval forces. It prepares them to fight and win wars and protect the country against threats. In addition to defending the United States, the navy also helps out when disasters strike around the world and sends sailors, ships, and supplies to provide humanitarian aid to those in need.

QUOTE

"It didn't take long for me to realize what an honor and privilege it was to care for America's warfighters and their families. Three years turned into more than 30 years and now I have so many fond memories of my time in the navy. I can't imagine a different career."

—Rear Admiral Tina Davidson, director in the US Navy Nurse Corps

GLOSSARY

amphibious
Working in both land and water.

anesthesiologist
A doctor who prepares patients for surgery by administering medication that makes them numb or unconscious.

blockade
A military act in which one state uses its navy to block supplies from entering a warring nation.

civilian
A person not serving in the armed forces.

deploy
To spread out strategically; to send into battle.

fleet
A group of ships that sails together for the same purpose and under one command.

gamma radiation
A form of dangerous electromagnetic radiation that is released when unstable radioactive materials decay into simpler materials.

GED
A General Education Development certificate, which proves a person's high school–level education.

humanitarian
Concerned with relieving human suffering.

hypothermia
A medical emergency that occurs when the body loses heat faster than it can produce heat, causing a dangerously low body temperature.

insurgent
A person who fights against a government or other authority.

intelligence
Information that is of military or political value.

marksmanship
The skill of shooting at and hitting a target.

mortar
A front-loaded cannon used to fire shells in a high arc.

optometry
The health-care field related to eyes and vision.

privateer
A privately owned ship that is armed and authorized for use in war.

propulsion
The act of driving or pushing forward.

rappel
To descend a vertical surface using a system of ropes and harnesses.

recruit
A person who has decided to enlist in the military.

schooner
A ship that has at least two masts.

secede
To formally withdraw from a political union.

sonar
A device for detecting or locating objects, especially underwater, by using sound waves that are reflected by the objects.

surveillance
Close observation or watch kept over something or someone.

turbine
A machine that uses a fast-moving flow of water, steam, gas, air, or other fluid to produce energy.

ADDITIONAL RESOURCES

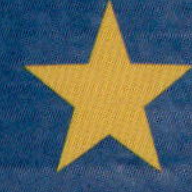

Selected Bibliography

"Get Started: Joining the Navy." *America's Navy*, n.d., navy.com. Accessed 23 Jan. 2020.

Kime, Patricia. "The Navy Is Gearing Up for 'Leaner, Agile' Operations in Arctic, North Atlantic." *Military.com*, 16 Jan. 2019, military.com. Accessed 23 Jan. 2020.

Lange, Katie. "Military Units: How Each Service Is Organized." *DODLive*, 17 May 2017, dodlive.mil. Accessed 23 Jan. 2020.

Further Readings

Lusted, Marcia Amidon. *US Military Special Forces*. Abdo, 2021.

McKinney, Donna B. *US Coast Guard*. Abdo, 2021.

Shoup, Kate. *Coding Careers in the Military*. Cavendish Square, 2020.

Online Resources

To learn more about the US Navy, please visit **abdobooklinks.com** or scan this QR code. These links are routinely monitored and updated to provide the most current information available.

More Information

For more information on this subject, contact or visit the following organizations:

National Museum of the American Sailor
2531 Sheridan Rd.
Great Lakes, IL 60088
847-688-3154
history.navy.mil

This museum honors the role of enlisted sailors in the US Navy. It includes historical exhibits and educational programs.

National Museum of the US Navy
1022 O St. SE
Washington, DC 20003
202-685-0589
history.navy.mil

This museum, located at the Washington Navy Yard, features historical artifacts and artwork related to the US Navy.

SOURCE NOTES

CHAPTER 1. RESCUE AT SEA

1. "Status of the Navy." *America's Navy*, 22 Jan. 2020, navy.mil. Accessed 22 Jan. 2020.

2. "Navy." *Today's Military*, 2020, todaysmilitary.com. Accessed 22 Jan. 2020.

CHAPTER 2. THE HISTORY OF THE US NAVY

1. "US Navy." *National Park Service*, n.d., nps.gov. Accessed 22 Jan. 2020.

2. "US Navy."

3. "US Navy."

4. "US Navy."

5. "A Brief History of USNA." *United States Naval Academy*, n.d., usna.edu. Accessed 22 Jan. 2020.

6. "US Navy."

7. "The United States Navy." *Encyclopedia Britannica*, 16 Oct. 2019, britannica.com. Accessed 22 Jan. 2020.

8. "Pearl Harbor." *History*, 6 Dec. 2019, history.com. Accessed 22 Jan. 2020.

9. "USS *Nautilus*." *National Museum of American History*, 2000, americanhistory.si.edu. Accessed 22 Jan. 2020.

10. "The United States Navy."

CHAPTER 3. THE US NAVY TODAY

1. "Status of the Navy." *America's Navy*, 22 Jan. 2020, navy.mil. Accessed 22 Jan. 2020.

2. "The United States Navy." *Encyclopedia Britannica*, 16 Oct. 2019, britannica.com. Accessed 22 Jan. 2020.

3. "Fleet Size." *Naval Vessel Register*, 14 Jan. 2020, nvr.navy.mil. Accessed 22 Jan. 2020.

4. Ed Grabianowski. "How the US Navy Works." *How Stuff Works*, 2020, science.howstuffworks.com. Accessed 22 Jan. 2020.

5. Michael Bame. "Understanding Different Types of Navy Ships." *Thought Co.*, 23 Nov. 2019, thoughtco.com. Accessed 22 Jan. 2020.

6. Bame, "Understanding Different Types of Navy Ships."

7. Rod Powers. "Frequently Asked Questions about Navy Assignments." *Balance Careers*, 23 Apr. 2019, thebalancecareers.com. Accessed 22 Jan. 2020.

8. Stewart Smith. "Things to Consider When Deciding Whether to Join the Navy." *Balance Careers*, 7 Dec. 2019, thebalancecareers.com. Accessed 22 Jan. 2020.

CHAPTER 4. AVIATION RESCUE SWIMMER

1. "Life Preserver: Meet the Navy AIRR Who Is Dedicating His Life to Helping Others." *The Versed*, n.d., theversed.com. Accessed 22 Jan. 2020.

2. "Life Preserver."

3. "Life Preserver."

4. Lori Rose. "Deep Water Challenge: Missouri Sailor Trained to Save Lives as Rescue Swimmer." *Brand Ave. Studios*, 17 June 2018, stltoday.com. Accessed 22 Jan. 2020.

5. Kirk Boxleitner. "Navy Rescue Swimmers Speak to Chimacum Students." *Leader*, 14 Nov. 2017, ptleader.com. Accessed 22 Jan. 2020.

6. Boxleitner, "Navy Rescue Swimmers Speak to Chimacum Students."

7. Boxleitner, "Navy Rescue Swimmers Speak to Chimacum Students."

8. "Melissa Dixon." *Today's Military*, 2020, todaysmilitary.com. Accessed 22 Jan. 2020.

9. "Melissa Dixon."

10. "Navy SAR Rescues Boater Off South Whidbey." *Whidbey News-Times*, 26 Mar. 2019, whidbeynewstimes.com. Accessed 22 Jan. 2020.

11. "2019 US Military Basic Pay Charts." *Navy Cyberspace*, 13 Aug. 2018, navycs.com. Accessed 22 Jan. 2020.

CHAPTER 5. NUCLEAR OPERATIONS TECHNICIAN

1. Thomas T. Charlton. "Life at NNPTC." *Joint Base Charleston*, 10 Dec. 2015, jbcharleston.jb.mil. Accessed 22 Jan. 2020.

2. Jennifer McDermott. "Women in the Military: US Navy Redesigning Its Submarines." *Navy Times*, 19 Apr. 2017, navytimes.com. Accessed 22 Jan. 2020.

3. "Navy Nuke, Submariner, and Saint Leo Grad." *Saint Leo University*, 2 May 2016, saintleo.edu. Accessed 22 Jan. 2020.

4. "Navy Nuke, Submariner, and Saint Leo Grad."

5. David Smith. "'My Transition' #27: Nick Reed Smith—Nuclear Submarine Mechanic to Process Manager at JBM." *Medium*, 19 Sept. 2017, medium.com. Accessed 22 Jan. 2020.

SOURCE NOTES CONTINUED

CHAPTER 6. CRYPTOLOGIC TECHNICIAN

1. "Leading with Regional and Cultural Expertise: Navy Cryptologic Technicians Go Beyond Linguistics." *Lead with Languages*, n.d., leadwithlanguages.org. Accessed 22 Jan. 2020.

2. "Leading with Regional and Cultural Expertise."

3. Travis Rose. "Cryptologic Technician Interpretive (CTI): Career Details." *Operation Military Kids*, 17 Jan. 2020, operationmilitarykids.org. Accessed 22 Jan. 2020.

4. "Navy Cryptologic Technician Collection – CTR." *YouTube*, uploaded by America's Navy, 17 May 2019, youtube.com. Accessed 22 Jan. 2020.

CHAPTER 7. NAVY NURSE

1. "Inside a New Navy Nurse's Life Abroad." *Villanova University*, 2020, villanova.edu. Accessed 22 Jan. 2020.

2. "Inside a New Navy Nurse's Life Abroad."

3. "Inside a New Navy Nurse's Life Abroad."

4. J. R. Potts. "USNS *Comfort* (T-AH-20)." *Military Factory*, 19 July 2017, militaryfactory.com. Accessed 22 Jan. 2020.

5. "Nursing Careers." *America's Navy*, n.d., navy.com. Accessed 22 Jan. 2020.

6. "Top Navy Nurse Describes a 'Typical Day' in Navy Medicine." *Navy Medicine Live*, 2017, navymedicine.navylive.dodlive.mil. Accessed 22 Jan. 2020.

7. "Face of Defense: Navy Nurse Serves to Make a Difference." *U.S. Department of Defense*, 14 Feb. 2018, defense.gov. Accessed 22 Jan. 2020.

8. "Top Navy Nurse Describes a 'Typical Day' in Navy Medicine."

9. "2019 US Military Basic Pay Charts." *Navy Cyberspace*, 13 Aug. 2018, navycs.com. Accessed 22 Jan. 2020.

CHAPTER 8. EXPLOSIVE ORDNANCE DISPOSAL TECHNICIAN

1. J. D. Simkins. "EOD Sailor Cleared a Daisy-Chained Minefield During a 10-Hour Firefight with ISIS." *Military Times*, 21 Sept. 2018, militarytimes.com. Accessed 22 Jan. 2020.

2. Kara Handley. "Women of Navy EOD: Ens. Brie Coger." *Defense Visual Information Distribution Service*, 22 Mar. 2019, dvidshub.net. Accessed 22 Jan. 2020.

3. James Clark. "There Are Some Things Only EOD Can Get Away With." *Task & Purpose*, 18 July 2016, taskandpurpose.com. Accessed 22 Jan. 2020.

4. "Navy EOD Techs Awarded Bronze Stars." *Military News*, 17 Sept. 2018, militarynews.com. Accessed 22 Jan. 2020.

5. Clark, "There Are Some Things Only EOD Can Get Away With."

6. "2019 US Military Basic Pay Charts." *Navy Cyberspace*, 13 Aug. 2018, navycs.com. Accessed 22 Jan. 2020.

CHAPTER 9. SONAR TECHNICIAN

1. David Hurst. "In the Spotlight: Under the Sea: Ferndale Grad Serves as Sonar Technician on USS *Maryland*." *Tribune-Democrat*, 13 Apr. 2019, tribdem.com. Accessed 22 Jan. 2020.

2. Hurst, "In the Spotlight."

3. Tim Miller. "Thomasville Native Serves at Sea Aboard One of the Navy's Most Advanced Submarines." *Thomasville Times-Enterprise*, 8 Nov. 2018, timesenterprise.com. Accessed 22 Jan. 2020.

4. Miller, "Thomasville Native Serves at Sea."

5. "Timothy Mays." *Today's Military*, 2020, todaysmilitary.com. Accessed 22 Jan. 2020.

6. "Timothy Mays."

7. "2019 US Military Basic Pay Charts." *Navy Cyberspace*, 13 Aug. 2018, navycs.com. Accessed 22 Jan. 2020.

INDEX

ABOUT THE AUTHOR

Carla Mooney

Carla Mooney is the author of many books for young adults and children. She lives in Pittsburgh, Pennsylvania, with her husband and three children.